BICYCLING THE

HOUSTON   AREA

A collection of 25 rides in and around Houston, Texas

R a l p h   N e i d h a r d t   &   B i l l   P e l l e r i n

Map drafting: Matt Luce

Cover art: Jan Zollars' Lamar Street Studio

Photography: Ralph and Bill

General assistance and encouragement: Many people!! Including: Susan Sternberg (Human-Powered Sports), Caryl Anselmini (help with printing), Dan Luce, Librarians at the Houston Public Library Texas Collection (historical research), the officers and membership of the Houston Bicycle Club, Inc.

To our wives;

> Dixie Neidhardt
> Lori Valencic

Published by;

**Texas Bicycle Map Company
P.O. Box 740981
Houston, TX 77274**

Copyright 1987, 1993 Texas Bicycle Map Company

First Printing, October, 1987
Second Printing, November, 1988
Third Printing, April, 1990
Fourth Printing, November, 1993
Fifth Printing, May, 1997

ISBN 1-882358-01-5

- INTRODUCTION -

It was predicted in the Houston Daily Post in 1892 that "Houston... for riders of the wheel will be a veritable paradise". Some may argue that this prediction never came true, but many others will argue that this area has plenty to offer the cyclist. Warm (often hot) weather, good roads, and a large variety of scenery are all within an hour's drive of Houston.

Welcome to a completely new book of bicycle rides in and around the Houston, Texas area. We have made an effort to include rides which will be of interest to all riders and we have indicated which interests are best served by which rides.

Some of these rides are ones which are based on rides used by the Houston Bicycle Club Inc. for its membership. Others of the rides represent new routes based on the experience of the authors and on many hours of riding and research.

There are rides in this book which, we expect, you would want to take at a leisurely pace. For those rides we have made a special effort to point out some of the sights to see along the way. We think that this information will enhance your enjoyment of the ride.

Other rides have been chosen to provide you with an opportunity to get a good cycling workout without having to drive a long way in your car. The scenery on these rides will not be as good as the scenery of the rides which are further from town, but we expect you to use these rides to get a good workout when your time is limited.

Most of the rides we've included require you to drive an hour or more out of town before you can get started. Your reward for this extra effort is that you'll be farther away from the Houston traffic and you'll get away from the coastal plain (into some hills). These rides combine nice scenery, interesting little towns, and sometimes challenging conditions.

While it is not the goal of this book to introduce you to Texas history, we couldn't resist including some historical information about the places you'll see along the way. After some miles of riding you might be interested in a tidbit of information about the place in which you've arrived.

We hope that you'll enjoy using this book and riding the rides as much as we've enjoyed putting this information together for you. We have tried very hard to make sure that the maps are complete and unambiguous, but if you find a turn that is particularly troublesome or have some new information which might be useful to us in subsequent editions, please write and let us know.

Thanks for purchasing a copy of the book.

- HOW TO USE THIS BOOK -

Selecting your ride

The maps are organized by direction from Houston, with the in-town rides given first. In-town rides will generally be shorter, more scenic, and more accessible. Other rides will require that you drive your car to the starting point and some rides will require more driving than others.

We have rated the rides on the basis of exercise potential and scenery/historical. Each rating is on a 1 to 10 scale, with 10 being the highest. The exercise potential rates the ride on its ability to give you a good workout. Some rides will have a low exercise potential due to higher traffic or more intersections (more stops required). Rides with a high exercise potential are preferred for exercise and training. Rides with a high scenery/historical rating may also be suitable as an exercise or training ride, but some riders may wish to take the ride a bit slower to take advantage of the sights to be seen.

Finding your way

Long routes - Follow the "L"   **Short routes** - Follow the "S"

Dirt roads - In a few cases dirt roads have been identified. This is to show you the road you should NOT take. None of the rides in this book include a dirt road.

Bike paths on in-town rides are shown with a dashed line.

UM - Unmarked road. Many country roads are not marked with a road name. To help identify these roads, estimate the number of map miles since your last turn (using the scale at the bottom of the map) and then, based on your estimated speed (or on an odometer reading) start looking for the road when you've traveled about the correct distance.

Sometimes turns and roads will be identifiable by **landmarks** shown on the map. On some maps we've identified some landmarks for you. We've also shown, in lighter lines, the roads which intersect the roads on the route. Often you can find the road you want by counting the **intersections** that you pass until you get to the one you want.

Alternate routes

Roads shown with a **double line** are generally **not recommended** for cycling. They have too much traffic with a narrow shoulder, etc. In some cases the route uses these roads when no alternative is available or when the shoulder of the road is adequate for safe riding.

Roads drawn with a **single line** (on out of town rides) and labeled with a road number are acceptable as short cuts for the ride shown.

Stores

When stores are few and far between, or when the town is small, the stores have been indicated on the maps. These stores will have all the basics: cold drinks, snacks, etc.

- SAFETY -

We urge you to **use caution** and to **wear a helmet.**

We have tried out all of the routes in this book but they are only as safe as you make them. Road and traffic conditions may have changed since this book was written. It is inevitable that some of the roads on these routes will have fairly heavy traffic. Be extra careful when you encounter such traffic. Watch out for holes in the road, railroad tracks (try to cross them at a right angle if possible), bumps, gravel, animals, and other cyclists.

Often, when a cyclist is involved in an accident the cyclist is at fault. Be vigilant, be careful. Wear bright colors during the day and wear white and use lights and reflectors if you must ride at night. Use all your senses, sight, sound, even smell if it helps. Many riders like to use a rear-view mirror on their helmet or glasses. Don't wear earphones when cycling. You might miss hearing something important (like an ambulance siren).

The best advice we have ever heard is, "Ride your bike as though you were a car in traffic." Ride where the right wheels of a car would roll. At an intersection take your place in line behind the last car waiting for the light. Never pull up to the light at the right of the line of cars. The drivers won't know what you are going to do. If you are in line with the rest of the cars the drivers will expect that you'll do what a car would do -- and they know what a car would do. After you get through the intersection you can pull over to the right to let the cars pass.

Stop for red lights and stop signs. Don't cut across corners. Watch out for obstructions (like speed bumps) in the road.

After all is said and done the responsibility for your safety is your responsibility. Most automobile drivers are courteous, but a few aren't. Watch out for them and give them plenty of latitude.

Laws

Bicycles are vehicles and, as such, are subject to the laws which regulate the operation of vehicles. There are some special provisions. One rule requires that you ride "as near as practicable to the right curb or edge of the roadway except when overtaking...". The law goes on to state that you are not required to ride into hazards (parked cars, sewer grates, broken glass, etc.) in an effort to comply with this provision.

"Persons riding a bicycle upon a roadway shall not ride more than two abreast..." and they "shall not impede the normal and reasonable flow of traffic on the roadway." Riders riding two abreast must ride in a single lane.

Generally, when riding with a group, we have found it good practice to switch to riding single file when one of the group spots (or hears) a car or truck coming from the rear. Usually, the first rider to see the car or truck will say, "Car Back!", and all the riders will move into a single line. The most common maneuver for switching to single-file involves the rider nearer the edge of the road increasing speed (slightly) and the other rider slowing and falling in behind.

- WHAT TO TAKE ALONG -

Water and Food

Equip your bicycle with one or more water bottle rack(s) and bring along some full bottles of water. You wouldn't believe how good warm water tastes on a hot day. Many cyclists bring bananas, bagels, apples, oranges, dried fruits, trail mix or other items with them on rides.

Tools and Spare Parts

Eventually you will have mechanical problems with your bike on a ride. This is why we recommend that you bring tools and spare parts with you when you ride. The stuff you bring need not be heavy or cumbersome and it will give you confidence that you can get home when your bike breaks (if you have practiced using the tools and making the repairs at home).

Tools

    Tire tools (for removing tires from rims)
    Spoke wrench (make sure it fits your spokes)
    Pump --Fits in the frame of the bicycle
            Be sure it fits the valve on your tube
    Adjustable wrench
    Allen wrenches (to fit the Allen bolts you have)
    Chain tool --small one
    Small screwdriver
    Small knife

Spare Parts

    Spare tube --dust with Baby Powder for easy
            installation
    Patch kit --be sure glue is not dried out
            and that patches are left
    Chain links --(just in case)
    Tire boot

If you were going on a 2 week bicycle tour you would want to take more tools and spares with you than this, but these items will see you through a day ride.

References

There is a good selection of books available on bicycles and bicycle maintenance. Check any large book store for these.

In addition, there are classes in bicycle maintenance offered by the Houston Bicycle Club, Inc. and by others. Check some of the adult leisure-time class schedules for details.

Contact the Houston Bicycle Club, Inc. at P.O. Box 52752, Houston, TX 77052.

- TABLE OF CONTENTS -

- In - Town -

- Downtown -

Start: *Anywhere downtown.*

Exercise potential: *3*　　　　　　　　**Scenery/Historical:** *8*

Recommendations: *Unlike all the other rides, there is no route specified for this ride. The idea here is to point out a few of the things to see downtown and let you make up your own route which will allow you to see the things you want to see. This ride is good for weekend or holiday mornings (before everyone else is up) ONLY! Downtown traffic on a work day could be a killer (literally).*

Riding downtown Houston can be a very enjoyable experience. There are lots of beautiful buildings to look at and sculpture decorates some of the buildings. Here's what's indicated on the map.

Allied Bank Building

[1] McKee Street Bridge & Habitat Park - *1923 bridge*
[2] George R. Brown Convention Center - *The center, which cost about $105 million opened the end of September, 1987. The city fought hard to get the 1988 Democratic National convention to come here, but the Democrats choose Atlanta instead.*
[3] Annunciation Church - *Oldest Church Building in Houston; Built 1874; dedicated 1871; steeple added 1881*
[4] Union Station - *Opened in 1910. Closed in 1974.*
[5] County Courthouse Complex - *The original log cabin courthouse was located on the site occupied by the present Harris County Civil Courthouse*
[6] Pillot Bldg - *Built 1858 Last Iron Front Building in Houston*
[7] Allen's Landing Park - *Originally the site of Houston's first port. The first ship to dock was the Laura which arrived on January 26, 1837. Southern Pacific railroad gave the land to the city for the park and with money gathered from private donations the park was developed beginning in 1966. For a while during the late 60's and early 70's the hippie culture (such as it was in Houston) claimed Allen's Landing as its own.*
[8] 200 Block of Main - *Interesting Interiors - Old Banks*
[9] Cotton Exchange Building - *Built in 1884 and restored in 1973. In 1874 the Houston Board of Trade and Cotton Exchange came to be.*
[10] La Carafe - *Built in 1845; The oldest commercial building in Houston*
[11] Market Square - *intended to be the forerunner to the shopping mall (that is a market square).*
[12] Christ Church Episcopal - *Founded 1839, built 1893*
[13] Lyric Building - *Sculpture - David Adickes - "Virtuoso"*
[14] Wortham Theater Center
[15] Alley Theater - *Opened in the present building in 1968. The Jesse Jones Houston Endowment donated the site for the building.*

[16] **Jones Hall** - *In March of 1974 Richard Nixon held a press conference at Jones Hall. When Dan Rather got up to ask a question he introduced himself, "Mr. President, Dan Rather, CBS News". Nixon knew (all too well) who Dan Rather was and replied, "Are you running for something?" Dan Rather answered, "No sir, Mr. President, are you?"*

[17] **Tranquility Park** - *In honor of the first manned landing on the Moon in 1969. The landing fullfilled a commitment by President Kennedy that this be accomplished before the end of the decade.*

[18] **City Hall** - *Located on land given to the city by George Hermann. Mr. Hermann's cabin supposedly occupied the spot now occupied by City Hall.*

[19] **Library Complex City Library** - *The old building of the Houston Public Library now houses the Texas Collection. Much of the information contained in this book was discovered in this building. On the inside the building is considerably more interesting and beautiful than the new building just behind it. The building was designed by William Watkin who also designed some of the buildings at Rice University (on the Universities Tour ride).*

[20] **Sam Houston Park** - *Purchased for a city park in 1899. At one time the park was widely used and contained a zoo. Now the Harris County Heritage Society is in charge of the park and uses the space to display several historical buildings. (See Parks Ride)*

[21] **Long Row and Texas History Museum**

[22] **Bob Smith Fountain** - *Wealthy oil man. Worked with Roy Hoffeinz to bring professional baseball (Houston Buffaloes) to the city in the early 60's.*

[23] **Enron Building**

[24] **Interfirst Plaza** - *Interfirst Bank Building suffered considerable damage (windows blown out) as a result of hurricane Alicia on August 18, 1983. Sculpture (a 3 dimensional painting, according to the artist) - Jean Dubuffet - "Monument to The Phantom"*

[25] **Allied Bank Plaza** - *Observation deck*

[26] **Tenneco Building** - *The Tennessee Gas Transmission Company (known after 1966 as Tenneco) was formed in 1944 for the purpose of operating a pipeline for the transmission of natural gas to the east coast. There was no interest in natural gas as a fuel before WW-II, but east coast demand made it viable to operate a pipeline for carrying gas after that time.*

[27] **Texas Commerce Tower** - *Sculpture - Joan Miro - "Personage with Birds" An interesting multi-color steel structure.*

[28] **First City Tower Plaza**

[29] **The Park** - *a downtown shopping mall. Busy only at noon during the work-week.*

Monument to the Phantom

[30] **One Houston Center**

[31] **St. Joseph Hospital**

[32] **Root Square Park** - *A hangout for the homeless*

[33] **Sacred Heart Cathedral**

[34] **YMCA** - *The biggest 'Y' in town. Location of the start of many 'fun-runs' in Houston.*

[35] **Whitehall Hotel** - *Fountain*

[36] **Chinatown**

[37] **Memorial Bike Path** - *Downtown to Shepherd*

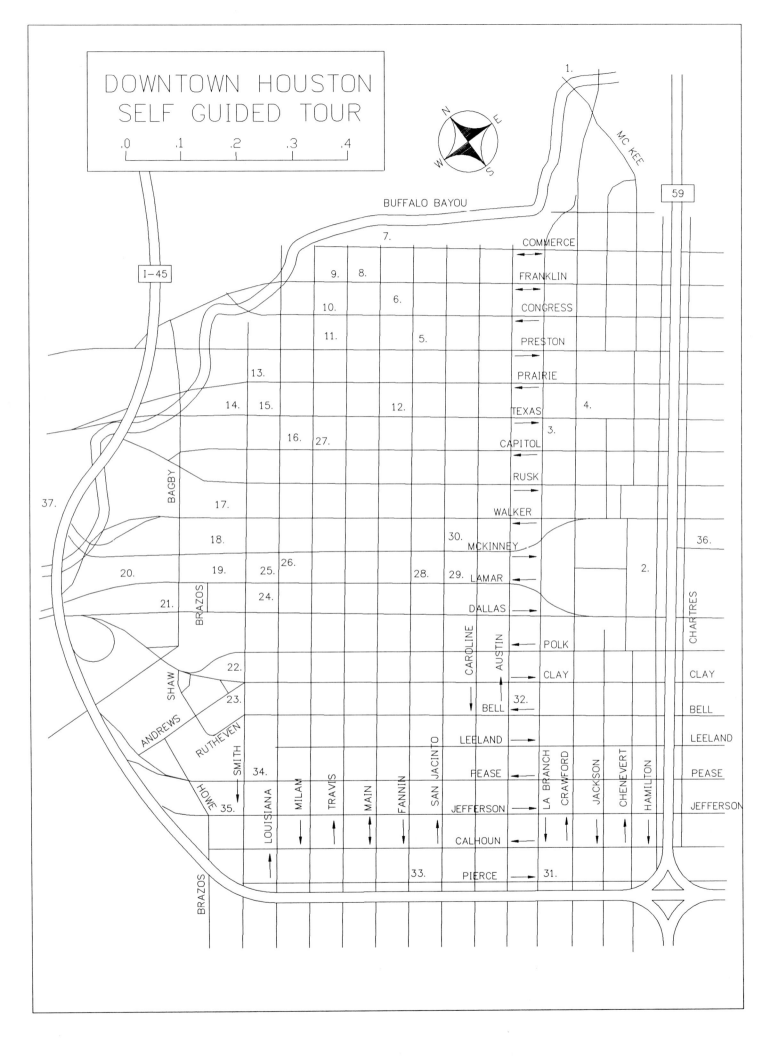

DOWNTOWN HOUSTON
SELF GUIDED TOUR

.0   .1   .2   .3   .4

- HEIGHTS - RIVER OAKS -

Start: *Northwest Mall parking lot. Northwest Mall is just outside Loop 610 at the northwest corner of the loop. It is between 18th street and Hempstead Highway.*

Exercise potential: *5*   **Scenery/Historical:** *9*

Recommendations: *Since this is an 'in-town' ride it is recommended for early Sunday mornings only. Houston traffic can be very difficult to live with at other times. May be some traffic on parts of 18th street; other streets should have light to moderate traffic.*

The Houston Heights - *has an interesting history. Before being annexed into the city of Houston in 1891, the Houston Heights was a project of a Nebraska land company whose cashier was a man named Daniel Denton Cooley. [1] Site of the Cooley home. Many beautiful, Victorian homes were built in the area including [2] the Milroy house, now being lovingly restored at the corner of Heights and 11th streets.*

The development was 23 feet above the level of downtown Houston and so the name Heights seemed a natural. Heights Boulevard runs almost exactly north and south and it remains basically unchanged today from its original design. On the 27th of November, 1892 the Houston Daily Post reported in its bicycling column: "The beautiful shell road at the Heights has served to inspire both lady and gentlemen riders, and there has been quite a number of additions to Houston's already large number of cyclists..." This shell was later replaced by bricks which are now covered by the pavement on which you ride.

The ride leaves the Heights and takes you to River Oaks. River Oaks is like no other community in the city. If you have the means (no other qualifications needed), there's no other place to live. No other place carries the prestige. The area is the home of many famous and infamous characters.

One of the most infamous stories is the one told in the book "Blood and Money" by Thomas Thompson. After Dr. John Hill's wife (house was at 1561 Kirby) died of a mysterious illness, Dr. Hill was charged with being responsible for the death. He was tried, but the trial ended in a mistrial. When Dr. Hill was later murdered, his late wife's father, Ash Robinson (house located at 1029 Kirby) was thought by many to be responsible; this was never proved.

River Oaks began in the 1920's as a Country Club community (with streets named after famous golf courses --Del Monte, Inwood, Chevy Chase) 3 miles west of downtown. It was intended that the community would offer houses which would be affordable to all classes but, as we know, it didn't turn out that way. [3] 1721 River Oaks Blvd H.L. Hunt had the house built in 1940 for his bigamous second wife, Frania Tye. Became "Carolina" in 1980. [4] Look for Shetland Ponies grazing in the front yard of this house. [5] River Oaks Country Club [6] 3376 Inwood Drive - house modeled on Mount Vernon.

River Oaks Country Club

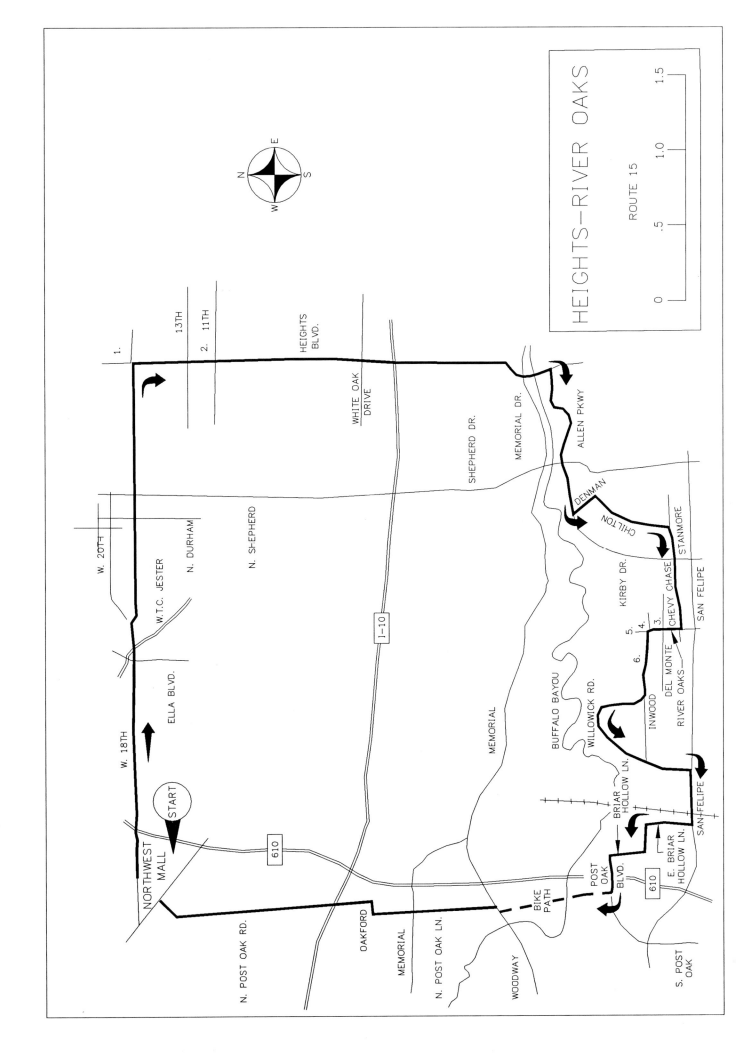

HEIGHTS–RIVER OAKS

ROUTE 15

0   .5   1.0   1.5

N E S W

START

NORTHWEST MALL

W. 18TH

ELLA BLVD.

W. 20TH

W.T.C. JESTER

N. DURHAM

N. SHEPHERD

13TH

11TH

1.

2.

HEIGHTS BLVD.

WHITE OAK DRIVE

SHEPHERD DR.

MEMORIAL DR.

ALLEN PKWY

DENMAN

CHILTON

KIRBY DR.

STANMORE

SAN FELIPE

CHEVY CHASE

DEL MONTE

RIVER OAKS

INWOOD

3.
4.
5.
6.

WILLOWICK RD.

BUFFALO BAYOU

I-10

MEMORIAL

BRIAR HOLLOW LN.

SAN FELIPE

E. BRIAR HOLLOW LN.

610

POST OAK BLVD.

BIKE PATH

610

OAKFORD

MEMORIAL

N. POST OAK LN.

WOODWAY

N. POST OAK RD.

S. POST OAK

- PARKS -

Start: *Any park on the route: Godwin Park (a few blocks south of Braeswood) at the corner of Rutherglen and Balmforth, Memorial Park, Allen Park, Sam Houston Park (downtown), Bell Park, Hermann Park*

Exercise potential: *6*   **Scenery/Historical:** *5*

Recommendations: *Another ride for early Sunday morning. (As you ride by Memorial Park you can wave to all the joggers sweating it out on the jogging trail.) Watch for traffic on Memorial Drive and on South Braeswood. Bicycle riding is not allowed on Memorial Drive east of Shepherd.*

[1] Godwin Park
[2] Transco Water Wall
[3] Memorial Park - *Before Memorial Park was a haven to joggers, tennis players, baseball players, and picnickers it was a World War I army training camp named Camp Logan. The property was purchased by Will C. Hogg, the son of Texas governor James S. Hogg, and was sold to the city at cost. Memorial Park is now the largest municipal park in the city and the largest urban park in Texas.*
[4] Allen Park - *Allen Parkway parallels Allen Park with its cycling and jogging trail. The name Allen is from the Allen brothers who are the founders of the city of Houston. In the middle of this park runs Buffalo Bayou. There is some question whether the bayou was named for buffalo fish which at one time lived in its waters or for bison which were rumored to have lived in the area. Each theory has its advocates, but the story about bison in the area has a bit more support.*
[5] Sam Houston Historical Park - *One of the houses in this park could be considered to be a*

Rice - Cherry House

pioneer version of a mobile home. The location where it sits in the park is the fourth location for the house. This antebellum (literally - existing before the Civil War) structure is the Rice-Cherry House. This house built around 1850 was sold to William M. Rice, founder of Rice Institute (later University) just before the Civil War. It was originally situated at the northwest corner of Congress and San Jacinto. Mr. Rice abandoned the house at the start of the Civil War. The house was used to hold Confederate war veterans during the yellow fever epidemic of 1867. It was moved twice before it came to rest at its present location. The first move took it to San Jacinto and Franklin, then it was moved to Fargo and Hopkins.

[6] Bell Park
[7] Hermann Park - *was named for George Hermann, a fellow who inherited some wealth and, through investment, acquired more. Mr. Hermann donated some land off South Main to the city for the park. The park has golf facilities, a statue of Sam Houston, the Burke Baker Planetarium, the Houston Museum of Natural Science, the Miller Outdoor Theater, the Houston Zoo, and a lovely Garden Center.*
[8] Braes Bayou Parkway

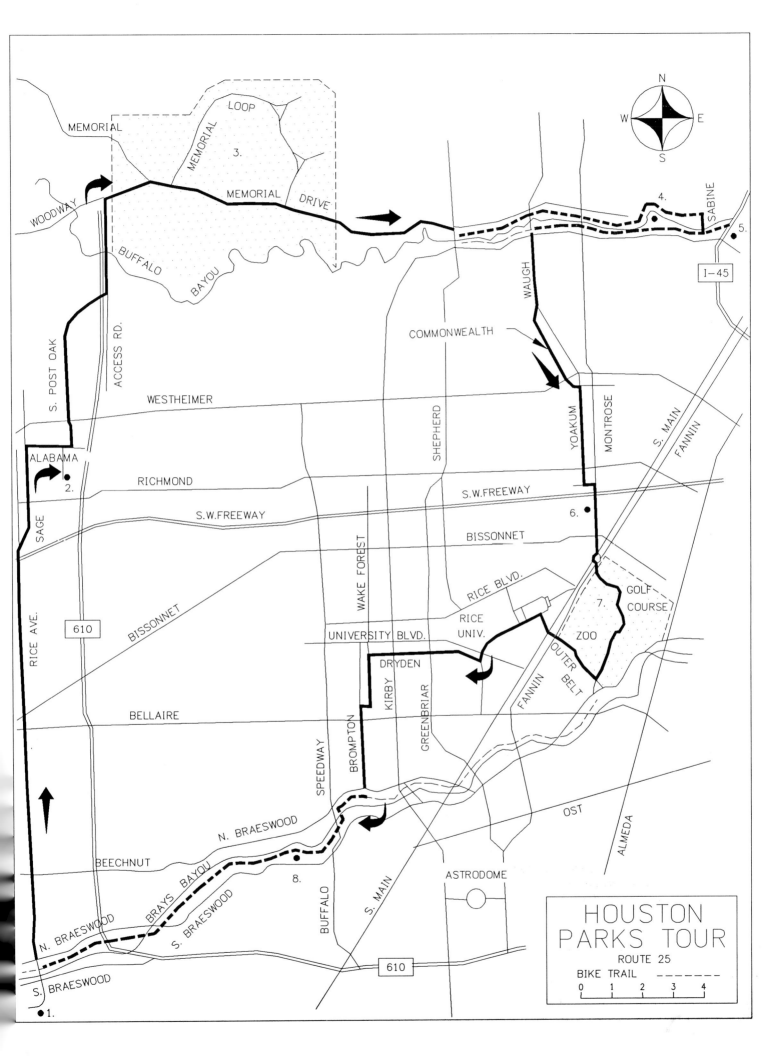

HOUSTON
PARKS TOUR
ROUTE 25
BIKE TRAIL - - - - - - -
0   1   2   3   4

Start: *Rice University Campus - (see location on map)*

Exercise potential: 6   **Scenery/Historical:** 7

Recommendations: *This ride is somewhat longer than the other in-town rides in this book. Since the goal of this ride is to visit the major universities in the city it is unavoidable that some rather heavily traveled roads are included. Take this into account and ride very carefully. Recommended for early Sunday mornings.*

Rice University - *Rice University is one of the 10 richest schools in the country. The school (initially Rice Institute) was chartered by William Marsh Rice in 1890. It was built in the Grand European style with many architectural embellishments. The school opened in 1912. Howard Hughes graduated from Rice in 1927.*

Houston Baptist University - *Houston Baptist College became a University in June, 1973. Columns from the Galveston County courthouse (demolished in 1965) were purchased by Theo Dora Heyne. Mrs. Heyne sold them to Stewart Morris, one of the developers and principals of the Nassau Bay and Sugar Creek residential developments. Ultimately, five of the columns were installed at the entrance to Sugar Creek and 10 were placed in the mall of H.B.U. The columns are 30 feet long and are in three 10 foot section. Each section weighs 6000 pounds and the crown weighs two tons. The courthouse was built in 1898 and was torn down in 1965 to make room for further developemnt of the county's courthouse and jail complex.*

Columns at H.B.U.

University of St. Thomas - *Rothko Chapel containing the last, brooding, paintings of Mark Rothko is on the campus. The works were purchased by Domenique and John DeMenil to be placed in the Chapel. A block west of here is the DeMenil Museum housing the family art collection.*

Texas Southern University - *T.S.U. is reaching mid-life, and if it is having any crisis you'd never know it. The school is over 40 years old now. It came to be when, in March, 1947, the state legislature created the Texas State University for Negroes. The first president of the university was Ralph O. Lanier. In 1951 the name was changed to Texas Southern University.*

University of Houston - *It was in 1935 that Mssrs William Bates, E. E. Oberholtzer, and Roy Cullen started gathering up the money they would need to turn what started as a junior college 7 years earlier into a full-fledged University. With some work and gentle persuasion these men were able to acquire 75 acres from the J. J. Settegast estate and 35 acres from Ben Taub. It was on this land that the permanent campus of the University of Houston was begun. School opened in the fall of 1939 with the Roy Gustav Cullen building completed.*

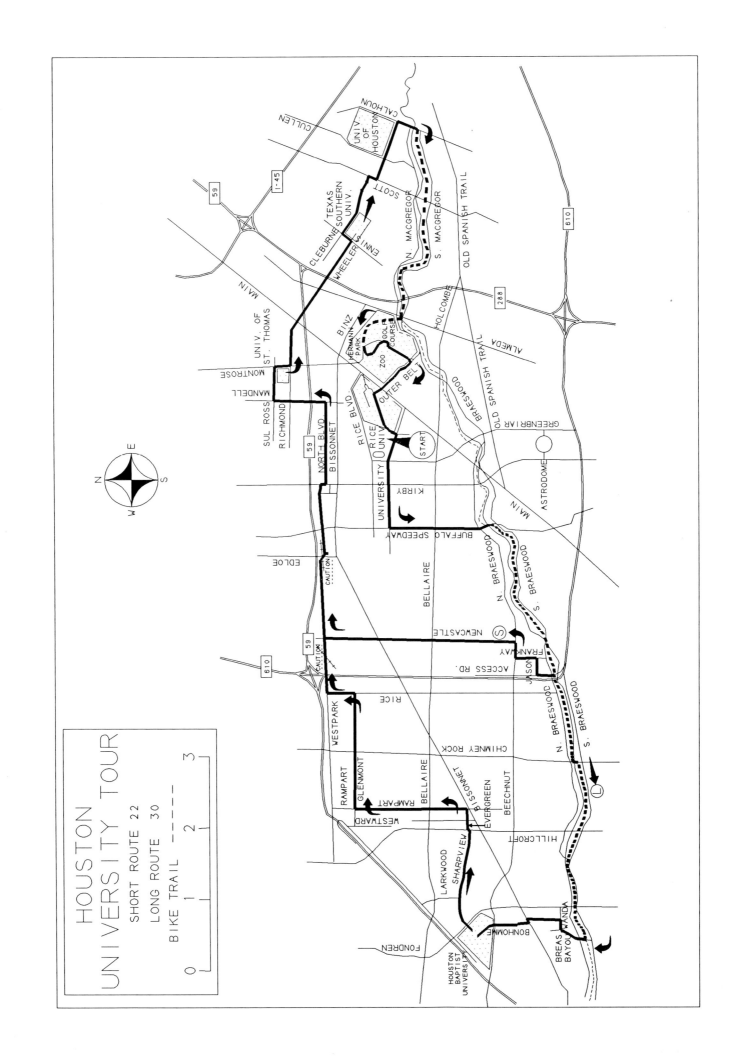

- North -

- CONROE -

Start: *Town square, Conroe. Take I-45 north from Houston 39 miles to Conroe.*

Exercise potential: *8*   **Scenery/Historical:**   *7*

Recommendations: *An excellent ride which takes you into the Sam Houston National Forest. Generally light traffic except near Conroe. The area is quite attractive to boaters on weekends. (Lake Conroe is 5 miles west of town on FM-105.) Look out for motorists pulling their boats!*

Conroe *- In 1885 the train tracks made it to the area now known as Conroe. By 1886 the area was known as "Conroe's Switch" in deference to Isacc Conroe who was running a sawmill in the area at the time. In 1889 Conroe was named as the county seat (Montgomery County) depriving Montgomery of the privilege. Oil was discovered in the area in 1931 (the height of the depression) by George Strake. In the 1930's oil was such a factor in Conroe that the area held the distinction of being the third largest oil field in the country. In 1964 (the year of the Beatles), I-45 opened a new path from Houston to Conroe.*

Microwave Tower on Highway 1097

Willis *- Peter J. and Richard S. Willis had been in business in Galveston when they moved to Montgomery County to manage their substantial timber and land holdings. The Willis brothers thought that the area would be suitable for a new town. In furtherance of this end they gave a right-of-way to the Houston and Great Northern Railroad. When the trains started coming so did the people. And so it was that in 1871 the town of Willis, ten miles north of Conroe, came to be. The ability of the town to service the farmers and ranchers of the area with shipping services and supplies for their continued operation assured the town of a continuing existence.*

Tobacco farming began near Willis in 1890 and the crops were so well received that they were awarded top trophy at the 1893 World's Fair in Paris. It seemed like a good idea that something should be done with the tobacco grown in the area and a facility for the manufacture of cigars was set up. Workers from Cuba were solicited. The workers wanted to unionize but the owners were not, as you might guess, in favor of the idea. The workers retaliated by rolling cigars with gunpowder in them. The net effect of this trick was the closing of the cigar plant. Exploding cigars were never a popular item. The Cuban workers returned home and Cuba got into the cigar business. (The cigar business in Cuba had its start in Willis?)

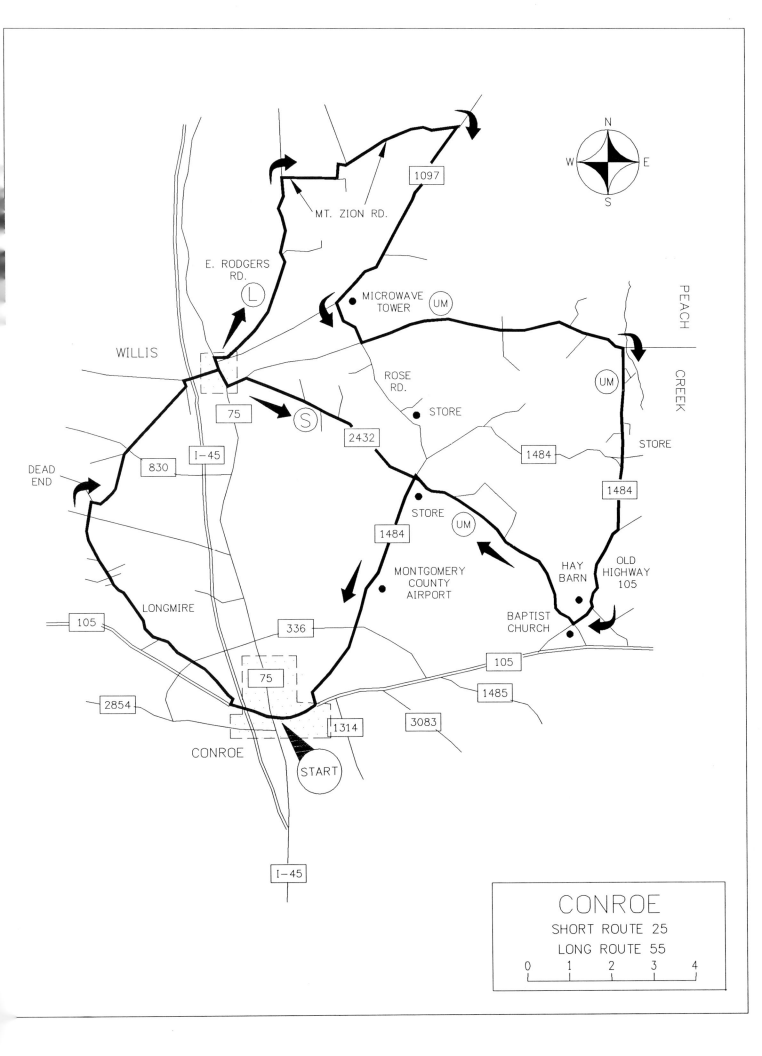

CONROE

SHORT ROUTE 25

LONG ROUTE 55

- NEW WAVERLY -

Start: *Just off I-45, New Waverly exit. Take I-45 north from Houston to the New Waverly exit. Just as you get off the freeway notice a little side road to your right. You can park here and start your ride. About 50 miles from Houston.*

Exercise potential: *8*   **Scenery/Historical:** *6*

Recommendations: *Great ride through the piney woods of east Texas. Watch out for traffic around Lake Conroe and in Huntsville.*

New Waverly - *is an outgrowth of the old town of Waverly. First settlers arrived around 1830. The area was a trading center until the 1870's when the townspeople refused to let the Houston and Great Northern Railroad run its north-south track through town.*

St. Joseph's Catholic Church - Rev. Felix Orzechowski came to Texas in 1866 in response to an appeal for Polish missionaries. He organized St. Joseph's parish in 1869 and established the first Catholic Church in Walker County. The large number of Polish families who came here in the 1870's were served by this church. Rev. Orzechowski left the church and returned to Poland in 1876. There he was imprisoned by ruling Russian officials for advocating democratic ideals. The present building began construction in 1905 and was dedicated on the occasion of the Feast of St. Joseph, March 19, 1907.

Huntsville - *founded by Pleasant Gray who came from Alabama (with or without a banjo on his knee) in 1835. He was reported to have said, "This is Alabama" upon arrival in the area and he named the town for his beloved Huntsville, Alabama.*

On September 4, 1841 Thomas Gibbs and Gardner Coffin started a little store which was to become the oldest continuous business in the state of Texas. The store sold groceries and general merchandise to its customers among whom was a Gen. Sam Houston. Mr. Houston believed in credit and a ledger sheet shows that he bought (on credit) 10 pounds of coffee for $1.00 and 17 pounds of salt for 50 cents. The Gibbs Bros. Building is at 11th and University Avenue.

New Waverly Catholic Church

Sam Houston built his home and plantation near town and called this project the Woodlands. Sam Houston lived his final years in Huntsville and he died there on July 26, 1863.

Huntsville is also the home for the Walls Unit of the Texas Department of Corrections. Visitors can buy prisoner handicrafts when the shop is open (Wednesday through Sunday).

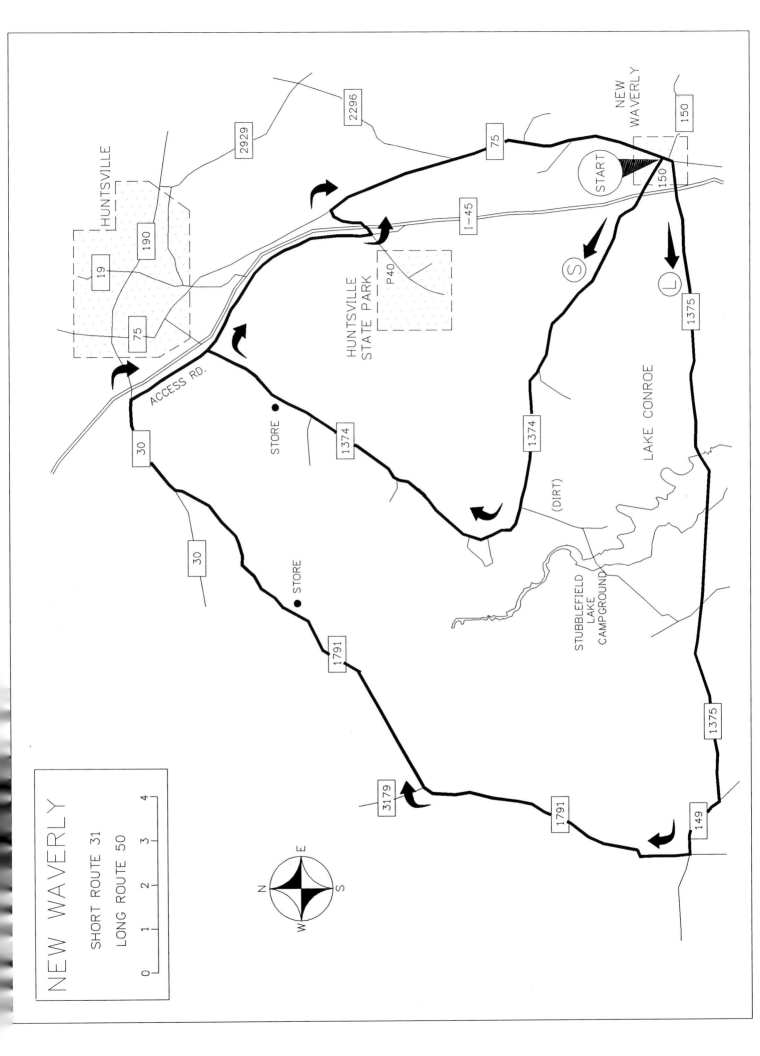

– Northwest –

- BRENHAM -

Start: *Blinn College campus. Take Highway 290 northwest to Brenham. Exit marked for Blinn College, turn right. About 75 miles from Houston.*

Exercise potential: *8*　　　　　　　　**Scenery/Historical:** *8*

Recommendations: *A very nice ride. A bit of a drive from Houston. Blue Bell ice cream at many locations in town.*

Brenham - *is perhaps best known as the home of Blue Bell Ice Cream (often promoted as the best ice cream in the country). Brenham was settled by German immigrants in the mid 1800's. Not long after its founding the town was occupied and partly burned by U.S. troops during the Civil War.*

Brenham can claim to have had the first tax-supported independent school district in Texas starting in 1875. Those schools and the members of the Washington County Grand Jury were the subject of bomb threats in 1967 when the jury began investigating allegations of the operation of a bawdy house on the road from Brenham to Navasota.

The investigation started when members of the Washington County Ministerial Association presented the grand jury with information relating to the nature of business conducted at the house. In fact, the business of a member of the jury was destroyed by fire. C.M. Hurst owner of Chappell Hill Electric Co. had received threatening calls prior to the fire and a strong odor of gasoline at the fire site was reported. In the meantime, a judge ordered Mrs. Eva Grace Long not to use her highway 90 property for immoral purposes. It turned out that Mr. Hurst admitted setting fire to his own property. His wife, two physicians, and the county judge committed Mr. Hurst to the Austin State Mental Hospital involuntarily.

Independence - *Just before you turn left from Highway 50 to Highway 390 you'll see the Baptist Church in front of you. General Sam Houston was baptized (November 19, 1854) into this church. The Houston family lived .3 miles west of this intersection. Across the street from the church is a small cemetery in which is buried Mrs. Sam Houston. Mrs. Houston died of yellow fever during an epidemic of 1867. Since the disease was very contagious it was necessary to bury her here rather than carry her to Huntsville for burial beside her husband.*

After you make the turn and as you climb the hill glance to your right. There you'll see the original columns of Baylor Female College. The school opened in 1846. For 40 years the college operated at this site. Men attended Baylor University on a hill to the south of this site.

Columns at Old Baylor

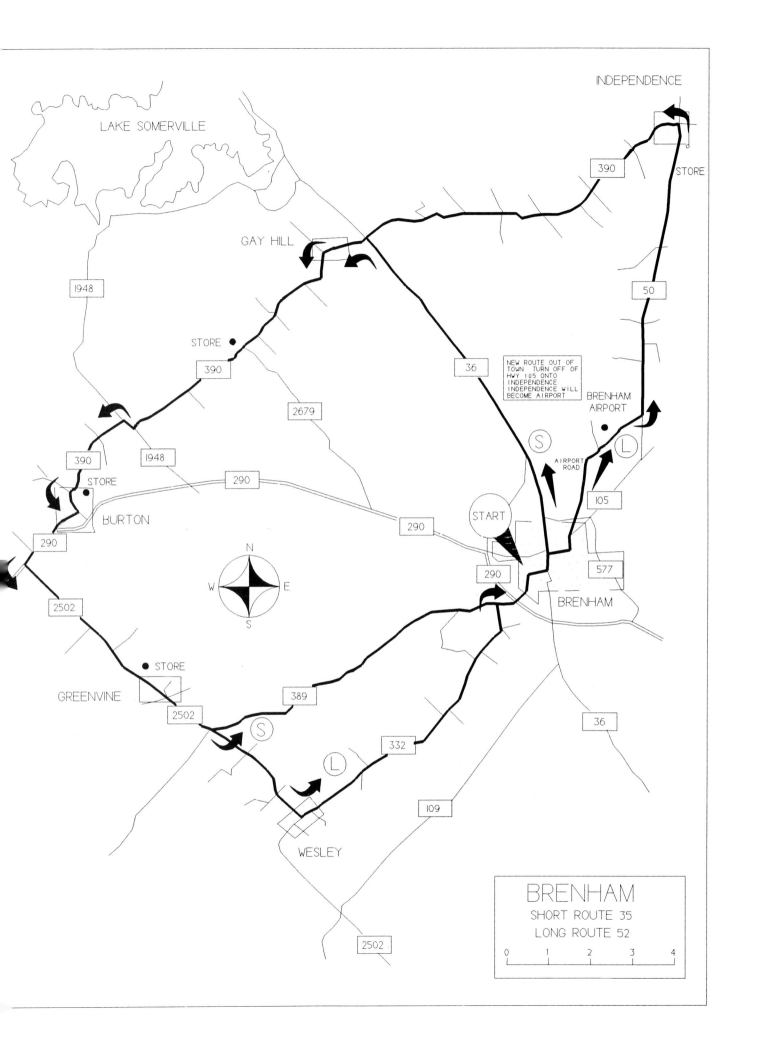

INDEPENDENCE

LAKE SOMERVILLE

390

STORE

50

GAY HILL

1948

STORE

390

36

NEW ROUTE OUT OF
TOWN TURN OFF OF
HWY 105 ONTO
INDEPENDENCE
INDEPENDENCE WILL
BECOME AIRPORT

2679

BRENHAM
AIRPORT

390

1948

S

L

290

STORE

AIRPORT
ROAD

BURTON

290

105

290

START

N

W   E

S

290

577

BRENHAM

2502

STORE

36

GREENVINE

389

2502

S

332

L

109

WESLEY

2502

BRENHAM
SHORT ROUTE 35
LONG ROUTE 52

0   1   2   3   4

- CHAPPELL HILL -

Start: *In the town of Chappell Hill. There's no mistaking the main street of town. To get to Chappell Hill take Highway 290 (the northwest freeway) from Houston. Chappell Hill is on 290 about 11 miles past Hempstead. 68 miles from Houston.*

Exercise potential: *8*   **Scenery/Historical:** *10*

Recommendations: *This is one of our favorite rides. It is challenging enough for hearty riders, but short enough for more casual riders. Half way through the ride you can visit Washington-on-the-Brazos historical park and get a break from your bicycle. On the way back you'll understand why the town you're going to is called Chappell H-i-l-l. The effort's worth it, though, for one of the nicest rides in the book.*

Chappell Hill - *was settled in 1847. It may be the only town in Texas designed by a woman, Mary Haller. Mr. Jacob Haller is given credit for being the founder of the town. Chappell Hill serviced many of the early plantations in the area and became an important education center in 1852 when the Methodist Church opened Chappell Hill Male and Female Institute. The Chappell Hill College for Women existed until 1912. The only thing left of the college is the college bell which was cast in 1873.*

Methodist Church Building

The Methodist Church was organized prior to 1847. The original church building was built in 1853 but it was destroyed by the great storm of 1900. The building was reconstructed in 1901. The church and the bell are located at the corner of Church and Poplar. Take Poplar east of town to view these sites.

Washington-on-the-Brazos - *your destination. It was at this site that Texans declared their independence from Mexico. In March, 1836 fifty-nine men came here to work on writing a constitution for Texas. There was an effort to make Washington the capital of the state, but that effort failed. When the rail line failed to make an appearance in Washington most of the townsfolk packed up and moved.*

There are several sights to see including Independence Hall, Star of the Republic Museum, Barrington (home to Anson Jones, the 4th and the last president of the Texas Republic). Anson Jones, by the way, was not in favor of annexation into the United States and he was quite disturbed when that happened. So disturbed was Mr. Jones that he came to Houston and committed suicide on January 9, 1858. He is buried in a graveyard off Washington Avenue in Houston.

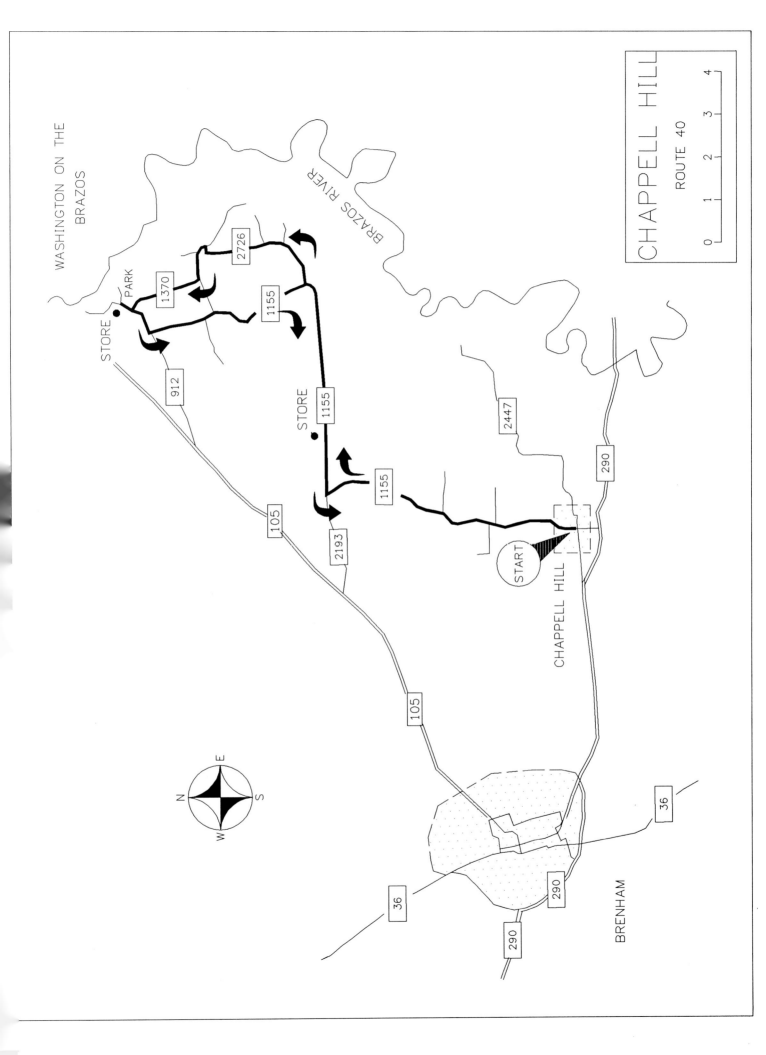

- HEMPSTEAD -

Start: *Hempstead town square (near the fire station). Take Highway 290 (Northwest Freeway) about 58 miles to Hempstead. When 290 turns to the right in Hempstead go straight and cross the railroad tracks. The fire station will be on your left.*

Exercise potential: *9*   **Scenery/Historical:** *7*

Recommendations: *Hempstead isn't far from Houston and this is a good ride, so it's worth the trip. CAREFUL: On the long ride there are few stores! Take plenty of provisions on a hot day.*

Hempstead *- Conductors on trains approaching Hempstead used to cry out, "Hempstead, Hempstead! Prepare to meet thy God". Legend has it that the three deadliest places were Hempstead, Hearne, and Hell. The place used to be called "Six Shooter Junction".*

When there was some disagreement about the issue of prohibition in Hempstead (1905) Waller County called a local option election. The people favoring prohibition won 777 to 654. The prohibitionists then called a prayer meeting for the evening of April 24, 1905 to give thanks for their victory and held it in the district courtroom on the second floor of the county courthouse. Skeptics advised, "If you want to pray, go to the church, if you want to get shot at, go to the courthouse." Before the meeting was over, United States Representative John Pinckney and his brother Tom, a storekeeper (both prohibitionists) were shot to death. Two anti-prohibitionists, who had come to cause

Waller County Courthouse

trouble, died also. Nobody was ever charged with any of these killings. The prohibitionists had little time to enjoy their victory; two years later another local-option election made the county wet again. The old county courthouse was torn down in the summer of 1954 and the new one was built on the same site.

Hempstead, founded in 1856, was named for D. G. S. B. Hempstead of Portsmouth, Ohio. The Houston and Texas Central rail line through Hempstead made it a significant supply point during the American Civil War.

Although we're not making mention of many eateries in this book, there is one in Hempstead that stands out - the Hempstead Inn. It is located on 290 as the road jogs north in the town. The Hempstead Inn requires a hearty appetite for admission. Food is served family style and you can have all you want.

When your ride is done and you're on your way back to Houston you'll pass a couple of farmer's markets on your way out of town; you can stop and pick up your veggies for dinner.

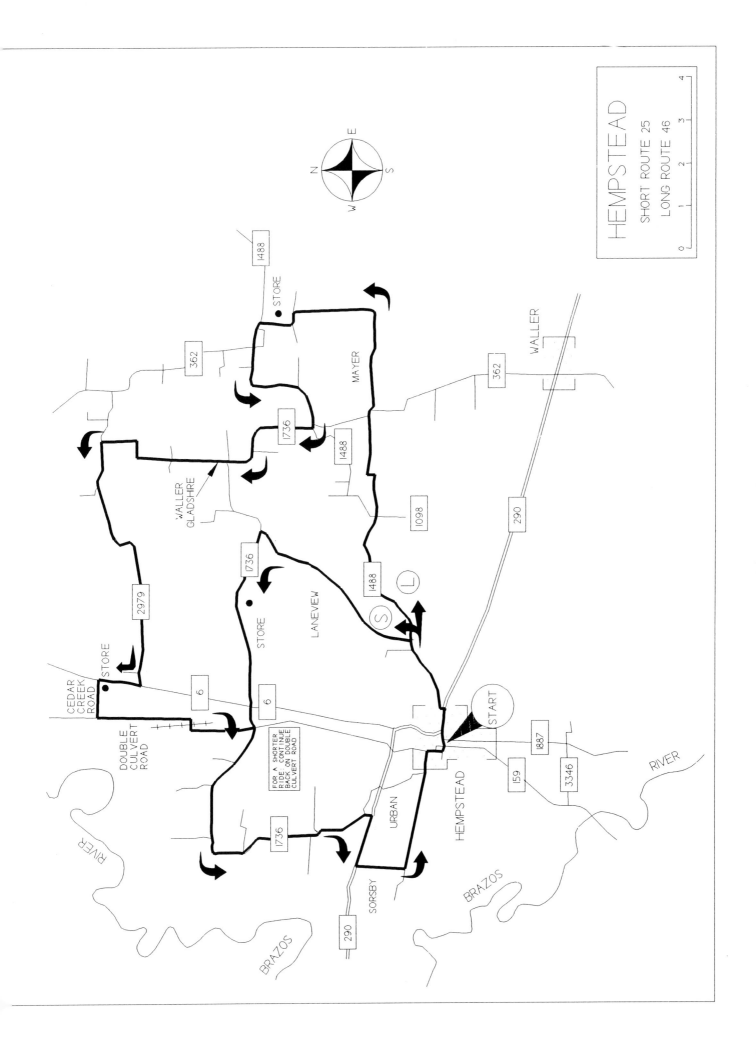

- MAGNOLIA -

Start: *The old Magnolia high school. To get to Magnolia take Highway 290 from Houston to Jones Road (just south of Highway 1960). Turn right on Jones Road to Highway 1960 (used to be known as Jackrabbit Road). Turn right on 1960 and drive to Highway 149. Turn left on 149 and keep going until you get to Magnolia. Highway 149 makes a right turn before you get to Magnolia. Ignore this turn and keep going straight (you're on Highway 1774). About a 55 mile drive from Houston.*

Exercise potential: *8*   **Scenery/Historical:** *7*

Recommendations: *Avoid this area on any weekend when the Renaissance Festival is on (generally October and part of November). The traffic will be heavy at this time. Otherwise, the area is gently rolling and wooded. Excellent riding.*

Magnolia - *There were at least four towns in the state of Texas named Magnolia. One was in Anderson county and was located about 10 miles southwest of Palestine. Another was in Eastland County, and yet another was in Montague County and was named after the Magnolia Petroleum Company. The Magnolia of interest here (in Montgomery County) was named for the prolific magnolia trees in Mill Creek (northwest of town).*

Magnolia had been the center of the largest sawmill operations in Montgomery County since 1927. But, in 1960 the Grogan-Cochran Mill shut down and about 200 workers were now without jobs. The mill was south of Magnolia on FM 149.

Montgomery - *Stephen F. Austin came to Montgomery to establish his fourth and last colony. The judge of Montgomery for many years was Nathaniel Hart Davis who built his house here in 1846. Judge Davis was encouraged to come to the area by Sam Houston who thought the area offered good opportunities for a lawyer. The judge created quite a sensation when he imported a 22 year old woman from the east to be his bride. She had traveled by river boat, ship, and stagecoach to get to Montgomery. The young bride was so well attired (with the best that could be purchased from Memphis stores) and the women of the town were so*

New Methodist Cemetery in Montgomery

impressed that orders for new materials from out of town were placed with the appropriate vendors.

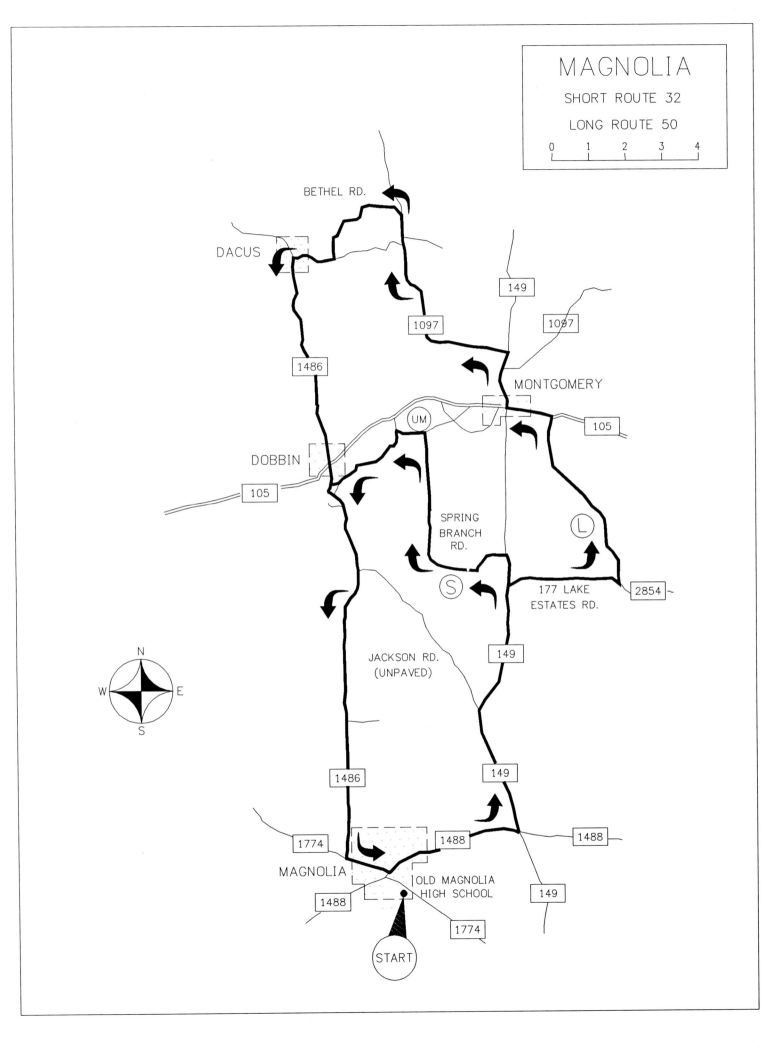

Start: *High School. Take Highway 290 (the Northwest Freeway) about 58 miles to Hempstead. Continue north on Highway 6 another 21 miles to Navasota. Take the Highway 105 exit. The High School will be on your right.*

Exercise potential: *8*   **Scenery/Historical:** *8*

Recommendations: *Good weekend ride. Low traffic on all roads except highway 90 (which has a wide shoulder). Plan on about 1.5 hours to drive to Navasota. On your bike, use the access road to get from the High School to Highway 3090.*

Navasota *- once promoted to settlers by Stephen F. Austin, is the starting point for this very nice ride. As a result of Mr. Austin's promotion settlers started coming to the area in the 1820's. By the 1850's the area was swarming with activity and construction of new and elaborate homes was proceeding at a rapid pace. The Civil War and a yellow fever epidemic took their toll on Navasota and the community never fully recovered.*

Anderson *- on the route, was once the 4th largest town in Texas. But, the railroad went to Navasota instead of Anderson and the growth of the town halted. The last vice-president of the Republic of Texas, Kenneth Anderson, died at the Fanthorp Inn and the town was named in his honor. Sam Houston often stayed in the Fanthorp Inn in Anderson (built in 1834) and drilled his troops in the front yard during the revolution. Robert E. Lee visited the Inn during the Civil War. There was a gun factory here at the time supplying weapons to the Confederate troops.*

The Grimes County courthouse, built in 1894 is visible from quite a distance out of town owing to the fact that the town is situated on the top of a hill. (Gear down!) The court house is built of hand molded brick and trimmed with stone from the area. In the 1930's a member of Clyde Barrow's gang was tried at the courthouse.

Grimes County Courthouse

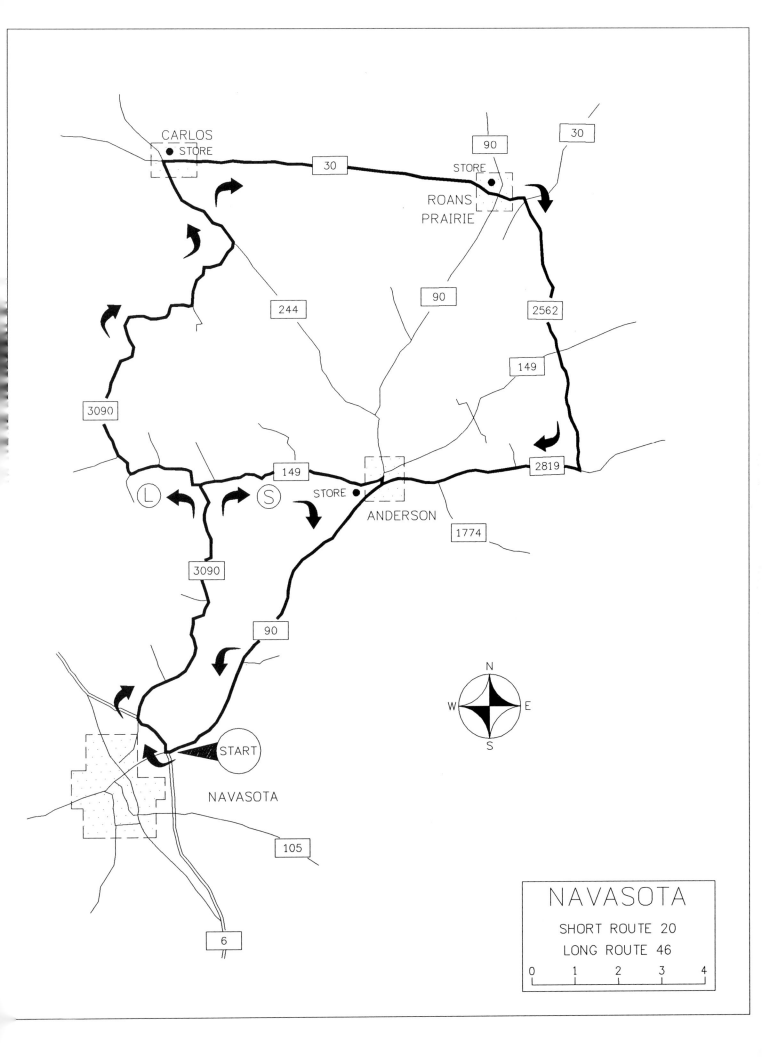

- West -

- BELLVILLE -

Start: *City park, just north of the town square in Bellville. Take I-10 west from Houston to the second Sealy exit. Go north on Highway 36 to Bellville. Turn left at the traffic light when you enter town. About 63 miles from Houston.*

Exercise potential: *8*   **Scenery/Historical:** *7*

Recommendations: *A very enjoyable ride in the gently rolling countryside just west of Bellville. Old Highway 36 is a bit rough, so be careful.*

Bellville - *Bellville (first settled in 1848) was named for a Mr. Thomas Bell, one of the Stephen F. Austin "old 300" (original settlers). It is now the home of the Bellville Potato Chip Factory, a Dairy Queen, a city Cafe, and a Pizza Parlor (everything needed to sustain life).*

The Bellville Potato Chip Factory located at 412 E. Main street is run by Wendell M. Ward and at this location the company manufacturers potato chips, jalapeno potato chips, various snacks, and tortilla chips. On the day we visited they were proudly showing off their new product: Designer Potato Chips.

In December, 1962 three jail inmates chipped their way through the wall of the Austin County jail in Bellville, slipped to the ground

Bellville Potato Chip Factory

on a rope made of bedding, and escaped. A fourth escapee was a young man, Archie Crowder, 19, who said that when he saw the hole in the jail wall he figured that it was "time to go home". His mother called to report the youngster had come home and he was returned to the jail to finish his burglary sentence.

Kenney - *in northern Austin County was established when the Gulf, Colorado, and Santa Fe Railroad built through the area in 1880 and was first named Thompson for J.E. Thompson, an early settler and postmaster. The name was changed to Kenney in 1890 honoring John W. Kenney. Mr. Kenney was a Methodist minister who moved to the area in 1833. He participated in the battle of San Jacinto.*

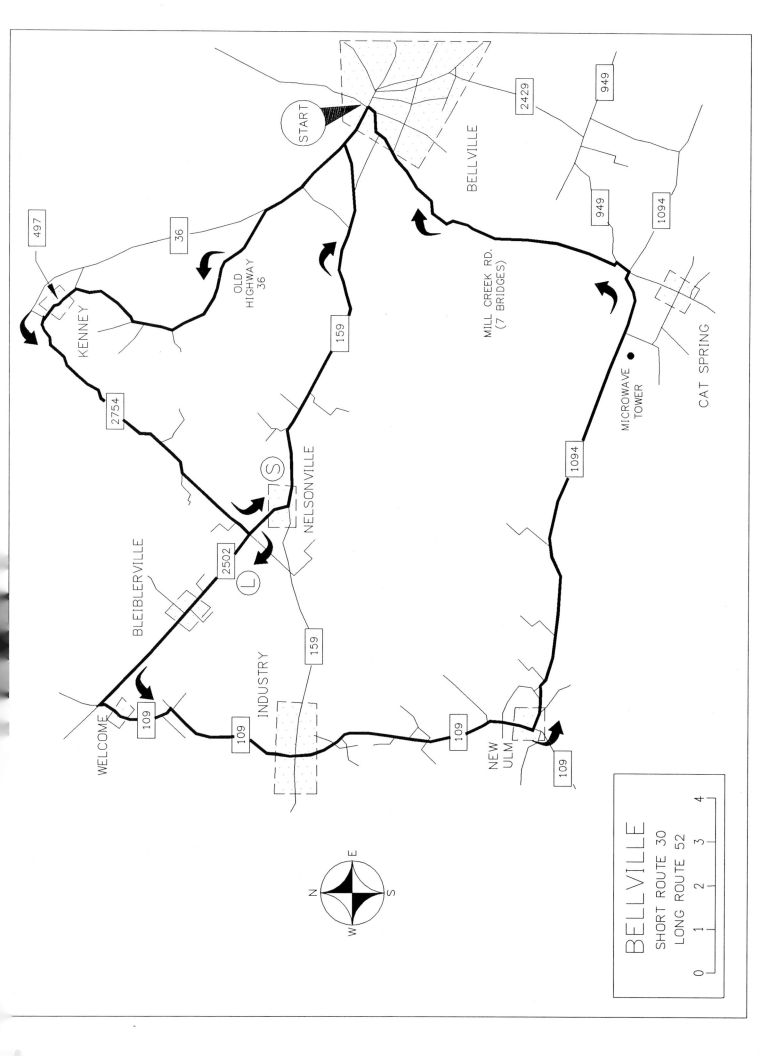

START

BELLVILLE

2429

949

949

1094

497

36

KENNEY

OLD HIGHWAY 36

159

MILL CREEK RD. (7 BRIDGES)

2754

S

NELSONVILLE

BLEIBLERVILLE

2502

L

1094

MICROWAVE TOWER

CAT SPRING

159

INDUSTRY

WELCOME

109

109

109

NEW ULM

109

N E W S

BELLVILLE

SHORT ROUTE 30
LONG ROUTE 52

0 1 2 3 4

- BROOKSHIRE -

Start: *Brookshire, Texas. Take I-10 west to Brookshire. Start your ride from any of the side streets in town. About 40 miles from Houston.*

Exercise potential: *8*   **Scenery/Historical:** *5*

Recommendations: *Excellent exercise ride without driving too far from Houston. Traffic generally light. Be careful crossing highway 1093 and highway 36.*

Brookshire *- (named for Nathan Brookshire) originally serviced the plantation owners in the area. The town provided the market and shipping point for the products of the area plantations and farmers. The Waller County Museum, housed in a building constructed in 1905 by Dr. Paul Donigan, is at the corner of Cooper and Fifth Street. The house is unusual because the good doctor insisted on the house having a basement. In a house so near sea level this was not practical. The solution was to build the basement at ground level.*

Waller County Historical Museum

Orchard *- (Fort Bend County) wasn't always as small as it is today. Even on a bicycle, a quick blink will cause you to miss the town entirely. The town was promoted, in 1890, by S. K. Cross and in 1894 the promotion was good enough to attract 27 families to move to the area from Akron, Ohio.*

Wallis *- Watch the railroad tracks in Wallis and note that these tracks are what allowed this little town to exist. So associated with the railroad was the town that it was named after a Mr. J. E. Wallis who was the director of the Gulf, Colorado, and Sante Fe Railroad when the town was established in about 1875.*

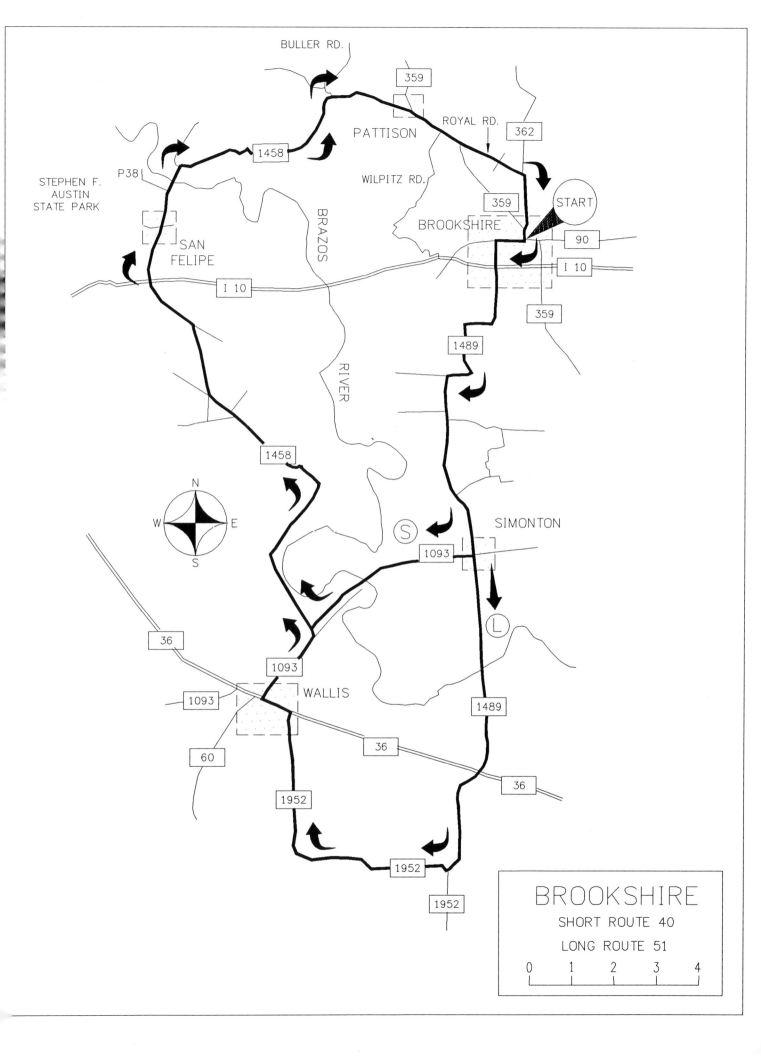

BULLER RD.

359

ROYAL RD.

362

PATTISON

1458

WILPITZ RD.

359

STEPHEN F.
AUSTIN
STATE PARK

P38

BROOKSHIRE

START

90

SAN
FELIPE

I 10

I 10

BRAZOS

359

1489

RIVER

N
W E
S

1458

S

SIMONTON

1093

L

36

1093

1489

1093

WALLIS

1093

60

36

1952

36

1952

1952

BROOKSHIRE

SHORT ROUTE 40

LONG ROUTE 51

0   1   2   3   4

- CAT SPRING -

Start: *Town of Cat Spring. Take I-10 west to Sealy. Take the second Sealy exit. Go north on Highway 36, cross the railroad tracks and turn left on Highway 1094. Go west on 1094 eleven miles to the crossroads. Turn left and go about a mile to Cat Spring. About 60 miles from Houston.*

Exercise potential: *8*   **Scenery/Historical:** *7*

Recommendations: *We have always thought of Cat Spring as the town that's just on the edge of the gently rolling hills to the west and the flat land to the east. On this ride you'll have the opportunity to get into some of these hills.*

Cat Spring Agricultural Society

Cat Spring *- This little village (Austin County) on the M-K-T railroad was settled by a group of German immigrants in 1844. Robert Kleberg is credited as the founder of the village. The name was given when Rudolf Von Roeder's son shot and killed a Mexican puma at the spring on their farm. Mr. Kleberg was born on September 10, 1803 in Harstelle, Westphalia Germany. He received a diploma of Doctor of Juris at the University of Gottingen. He married Rosa von Roeder and joined a group of immigrants leaving Germany on Sept. 30, 1834. The vessel on which they traveled was wrecked off Galveston Island in December, 1834 and Kleberg and Louis von Roeder went on foot from Brazoria, Tx to San Felipe. The family settled near the location of Cat Spring in the fall of 1835. Kleberg served in the Texas Army from March 25 to July 23, 1835 and participated in the battle of San Jacinto. During the time the family had moved from their home in Cat Spring their home was ravaged and lost. After the war Kleberg settled in Galveston but he later returned to Austin County. He became justice of the peace of Austin County.*

The first agricultural society in Texas was organized by the German inhabitants at Cat Spring in 1856. The Cat Spring Agricultural Society building is just west of the intersection of FM-1094 and FM-949. This building was originally constructed in 1902 and it is still being used. The Society maintained crop records and made these records available to other farmers in the area to assist in their endeavors. The German language was often used at the Society meetings.

Bernardo *- Originally the site of a plantation home, the area can also claim to be the site of Sam Houston's encampment on his way to San Jacinto. General Houston camped here for 2 weeks training his army before marching on toward San Jacinto. Groce's Plantation, nearby was the site. The army grew to approximately 1400 men.*

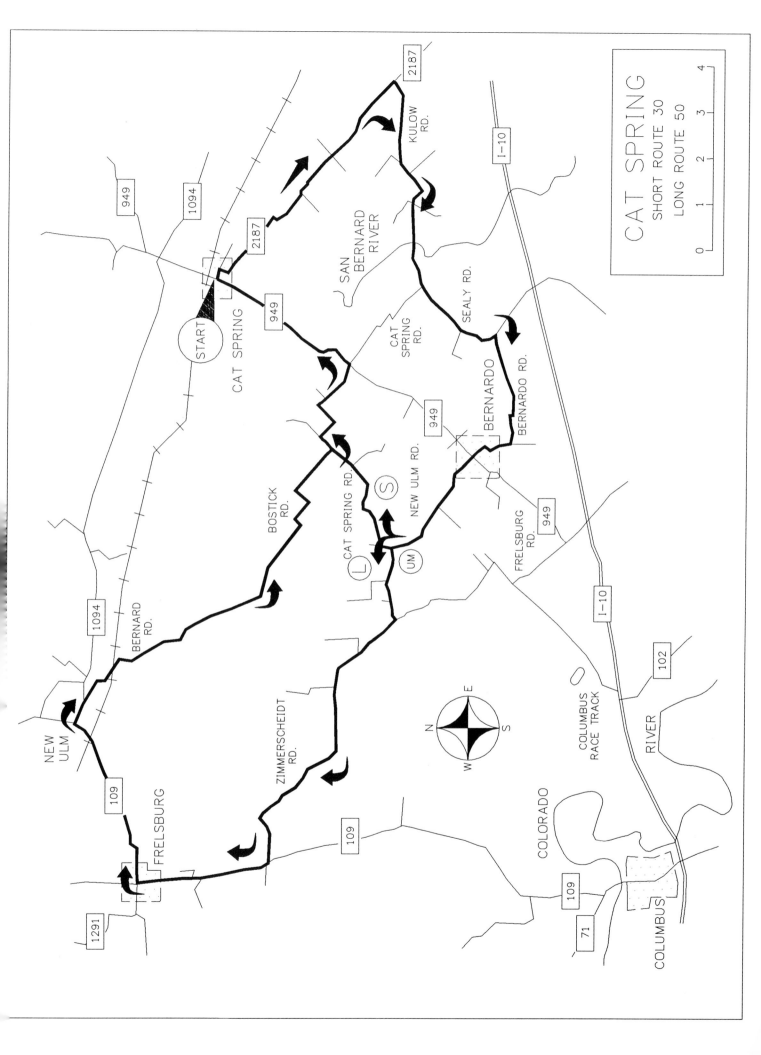

CAT SPRING
SHORT ROUTE 30
LONG ROUTE 50

START

CAT SPRING

949

949

1094

2187

KULOW RD.

SAN BERNARD RIVER

SEALY RD.

CAT SPRING RD.

BERNARDO

BERNARDO RD.

I-10

949

FRELSBURG RD.

I-10

102

NEW ULM RD.

CAT SPRING RD.

S

L

UM

BOSTICK RD.

BERNARD RD.

1094

NEW ULM

109

FRELSBURG

1291

ZIMMERSCHEIDT RD.

109

COLUMBUS RACE TRACK

COLORADO

RIVER

109

71

COLUMBUS

N
W   E
S

0   1   2   3   4

- COLUMBUS -

Start: *Town of Columbus on the town square. 70 Miles west of Houston on IH-10.*

Exercise potential: *9*   **Scenery/Historical:** *8*

Recommendations: *Beautiful ride through the countryside around Columbus. Zimmerscheidt Road is especially nice. Be very careful leaving town. You have to cross the Colorado River bridge on your way out and it's not got a lot of extra room! There's another bridge to cross as you come back into town from the south. Be careful on that one too. Otherwise, traffic is generally light.*

Columbus - *When settlers came to Texas they came first to the area around Columbus. Stephen F. Austin originally intended that this settlement would become the capitol of the colony, but settlers in this area were under constant threat of attack from the Karankawa Indians and more colonists settled on the Brazos River. So, the capitol was never established at Columbus. The town was known to the settlers as Beason's Ferry when they began creating formal plans for the town in 1835. It was only a year later that Sam Houston and his troops, in retreat from Gonzales, camped in Columbus. Sam Houston's little army was outnumbered by Santa Anna's army which was camped near-by. He had no choice but to order the town destroyed. He then moved his troops east, ultimately to San Jacinto and victory.*

When you park your car in Columbus take a minute to view the large Oak tree (or what's left of it) on the end of the town square. Judge Williamson (also known as Three-Legged Willie due to a childhood bout with polio) made it his responsibility to bring law and order to the area. And not just any law and order would do. Judge Williamson insisted on the law and order as proscribed by the Texas Constitution which had been only recently made the law of the state. The citizens could do nothing but accept the authority of Three Legged Willie.

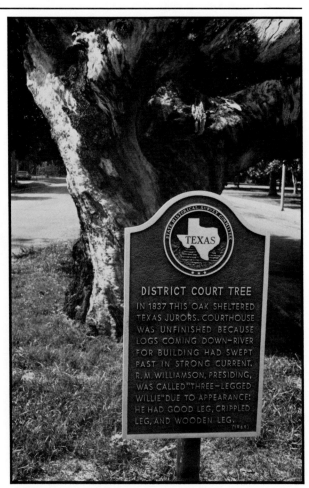

District Court Tree

Lone Oak - *You're probably wondering where the clever name for this town came from. The story is that when the M-K-T(Katy) railroad was coming through the area the only way to identify the place was by a 'lone oak' tree that was near the rail line.*

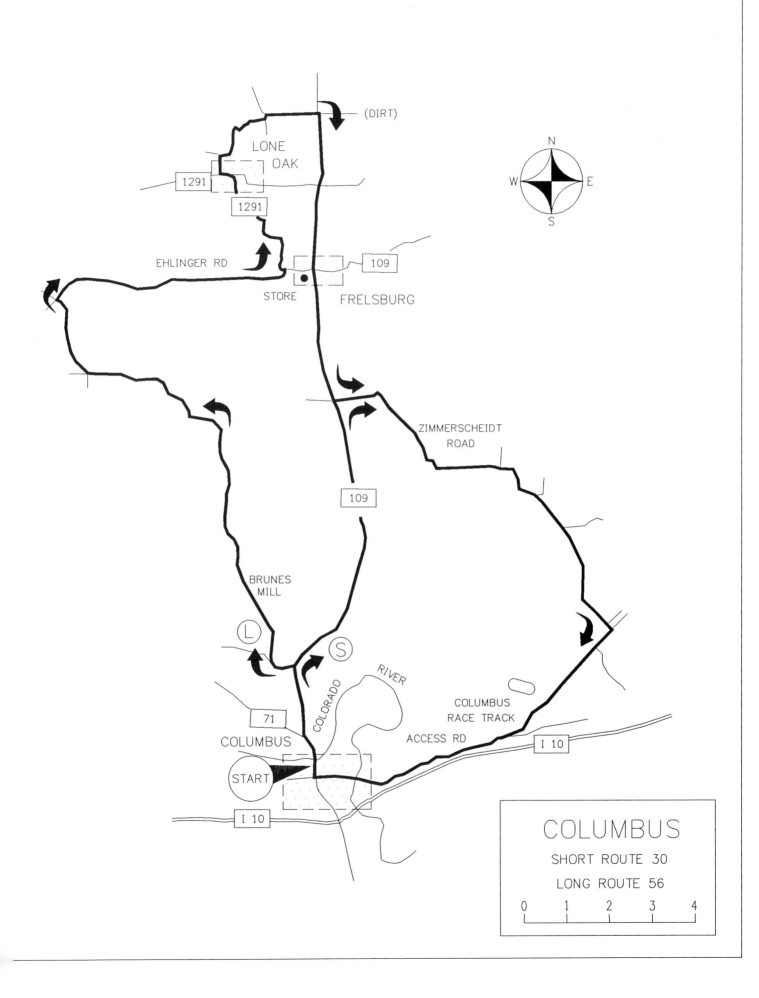

(DIRT)

LONE OAK

1291

1291

EHLINGER RD

109

STORE   FRELSBURG

ZIMMERSCHEIDT ROAD

109

BRUNES MILL

L

S

COLORADO RIVER

71

COLUMBUS

COLUMBUS RACE TRACK

ACCESS RD

I 10

START

I 10

N
W   E
S

COLUMBUS

SHORT ROUTE 30

LONG ROUTE 56

0   1   2   3   4

- FAYETTEVILLE -

Start: *Town Square in Fayetteville. Take I-10 west from Houston to second Sealy exit. Go north on Highway 36 to Highway 1094. Go west on 1094 twenty-two miles to New Ulm. When the road ends go left on Highway 109 to Frelsburg. Continue past Frelsburg. Bear right on Highway 1291 and continue to Fayetteville. About 85 miles from Houston.*

Exercise potential: *10*   **Scenery/Historical:** *8*

Recommendations: *Excellent ride! A long drive from Houston. Watch out for fairly heavy traffic on highway 159. Wide shoulder on that road helps.*

Fayetteville *- was first settled in the 1820's by members of Stephen F. Austin's Old 300. These first settlers were mostly of German, Bohemian, and Moravian descent.*

You'd guess that the town of Fayetteville was named for Fayette County, but you'd be wrong. It was named in favor of Fayetteville, North Carolina, birthplace of the man who laid out the town in 1844 - Phil Shaver. Before, it was called Lickskillet; before that, Alexander's Voting Place; before that, Wadis Post Office. Using one of its earlier monikers (in 1833) this was an important station on the San Felipe-Bastrop Stage line.

Every town should have at least one claim to fame. Fayetteville's is its town clock. It is significant because Fayetteville is mentioned in "Ripley's Believe it or Not" as the smallest town in the United States to have a town clock. The clock has faces on all four sides and it was manufactured by the Seth Thomas company. It was in 1934 that the Do Your Duty Club (a group of ladies who gave dances and sold kolaches for 10 years) announced that they had raised enough money to buy the clock.

Fayetteville   Courthouse

The courthouse was built in 1880 and it has the interesting feature of being built with very few nails. Most of the structural members are mortised. The first floor of the building is a large meeting room with a rostrum (the rest room is outside), benches, and a wood stove. The second story originally housed two wooden jail cells but these haven't been used for a long time.

Warrenton *- William Neese landed in Galveston in December, 1847 and opened a store at the site of Warrenton. The town was finally named for Warren Ligon, an early settler in the area. Joel Walter Robison lived two miles from Warrenton. He distinguished himself by being one of the men who captured Antonio Lopez de Santa Anna at the battle of San Jacinto.*

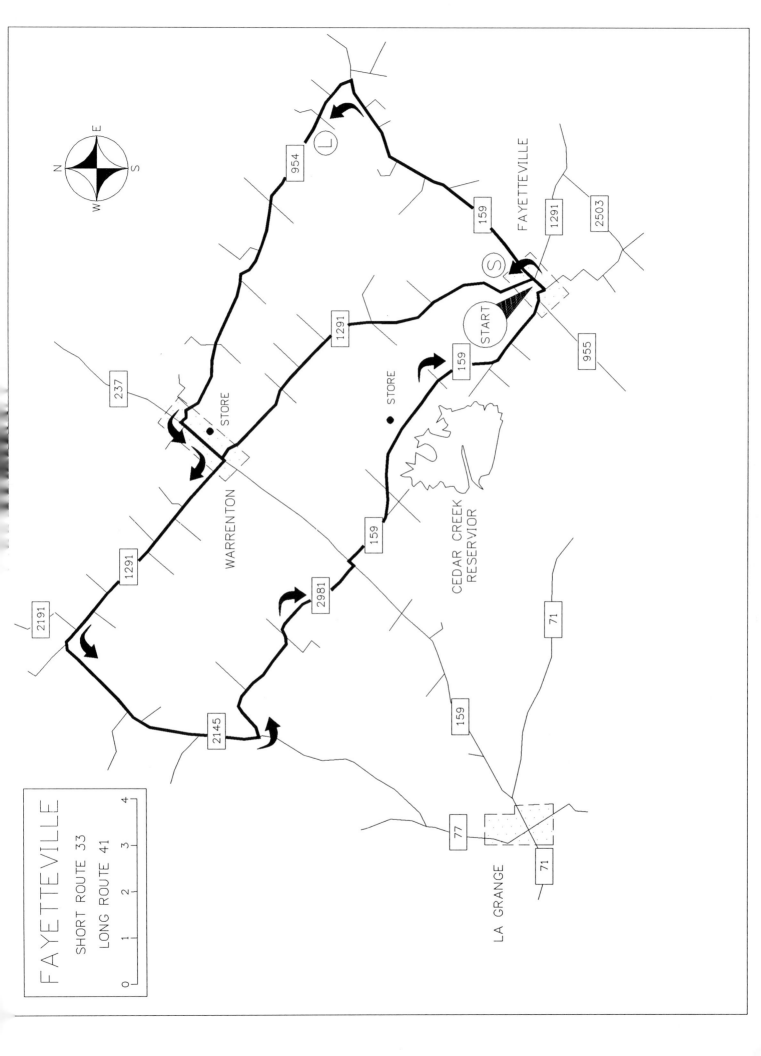

- KATY -

Start: *Katy High School on Highway 90 in Katy. Take I-10 west to the first Katy exit. Continue on Highway 90 through town to the High School. About 30 miles from Houston.*

Exercise potential: *8*   **Scenery/Historical:** *4*

Recommendations: *A good ride for the cyclist who is out for a good exercise and training ride. Close to Houston. Flat land with not too much traffic (be careful on 1093, 359, and 529 - these roads could be a bit busy). No hills. Great bar-b-que stop at Doziers in Fulshear.*

Katy - *The first train that entered the state of Texas entered on a rail line owned by the Missouri-Kansas-Texas Railroad. The M-K-T railroad was known as the Katy (K-T) Railroad and the town is, at least in the most often heard story, named after this railroad. There's another story that has some credence, however. Some folks say that the town wasn't named after the railroad at all; it was named after a Ms Katie Mares who was the local saloon keeper in the area during the time when the railroad was going in (early 1890's). According to this story the track laying gangs would often end their day with the suggestion, "Let's go to Katie for a beer".*

By 1901 the K-T railroad line had extended to San Antonio and by 1904 it was in Austin.

The area around Katy was first settled about 1852 when a stagecoach stop was established by Cane Island Creek (which empties into Buffalo Bayou). The location was handy because it was half the way from Sealy to Houston. The stagecoach quit running in 1875 when a narrow gauge railroad connected Pattison, Sealy, and Houston.

Old Katy Rail Station

Fulshear - *The southern end of this ride is the little village of Fulshear. The community began near Hady Creek and it was named for Churchill Fulshear, one of Stephen F. Austin's Old 300. Churchill Fulshear came from Tennessee to Texas and received title to land in what is now Fort Bend County. Fulshear did not live to see the Texas Revolution, but his three sons and his one daughter did and his plantation was used for the headquarters of the Texas soldiers commanded by Wylie Martin. The town of Fulshear was established in 1890 when the Texas and New Orleans Railroad was built.*

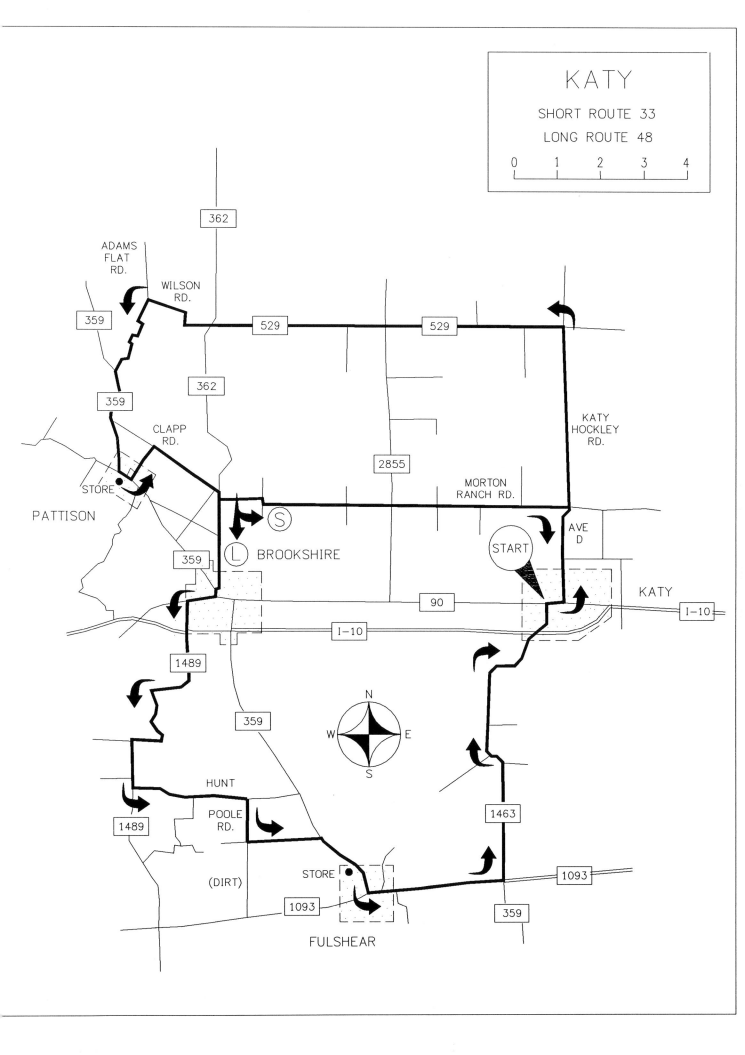

Start: *Town of New Ulm. Take I-10 west to Sealy. Take the second Sealy exit. Go north on Highway 36, cross the railroad tracks, and turn left on Highway 1094. Go west on 1094 twenty-two miles to New Ulm. About 70 miles from Houston.*

Exercise potential: *9*   **Scenery/Historical:** *8*

Recommendations: *Just about as good a ride as you can get in the Houston area (and that's pretty good). Excellent roads, light traffic and enough hills to make the ride interesting. A bit of a drive from Houston, but if you have the time you'll be amply rewarded.*

New Ulm - *is on the M-K-T railroad in western Austin County. The area was known first as Duff's Settlement in deference to James C. Duff. Mr. Duff had been granted the land in 1841. By the mid 1800's the little town was more established and it was renamed by its*

The Parlour

mostly German settlers for the city of Ulm in Wurttemberg, Germany. New Ulm had a flurry of activity in the late 1940's when Glenn McCarthy ignited an oil rush there. The oil boom fizzled when it was discovered that the oil field was too shallow to produce.

The building now housing the Parlour Restuarant in New Ulm had once housed the town funeral parlor. The building survived the 1900 storm that devastated Galveston because holes were drilled in the floor to prevent the rising water from lifting the structure off its foundation.

Industry - *was the first permanent German colony founded in Texas. Friedrich Ernst and Charles Fordtran were immigrants from Germany who came to New York, moved to New Orleans, and then (having been sold on the idea of coming to one of Stephen F. Austin's colonies) decided to come to Texas. Ernst and Fordtran divided a league (4428.4 acres) of land near Mill Creek on April 16, 1831. So enthusiastic were Ernst and Fordtran that they composed letters to Germany persuading other families to immigrate and move to Industry in 1833 and 1834. Many of the new, German, residents suggested that Mr. Ernst make cigars from the tobacco grown in his garden. The cigar making industry which ultimately developed was responsible for the name Industry being attached to the town.*

Frelsberg - *was named for John and William Frels who settled the area in the 1830's. The Frelsburg Church of Sts. Peter and Paul (just south of town) is associated with the oldest parish in the state of Texas. Heinsohn's General Store is a good stop on a hot day. Plenty of cold drinks and lots more.*

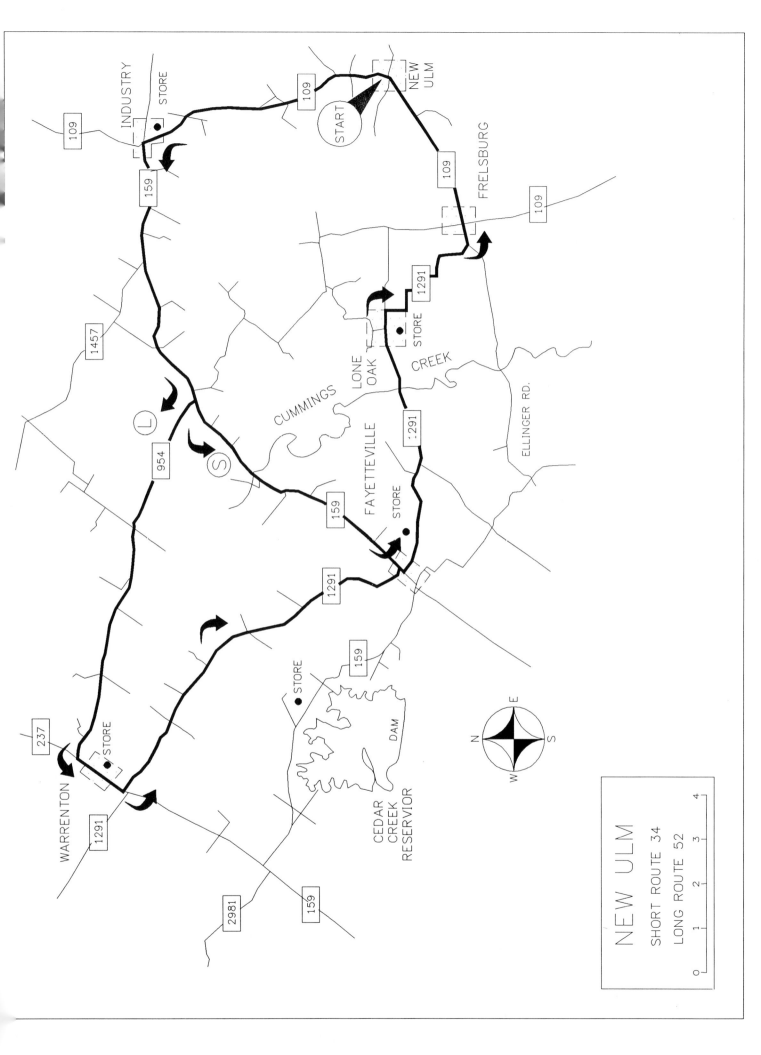

NEW ULM

SHORT ROUTE 34
LONG ROUTE 52

0 1 2 3 4

- SEALY -

Start: *The city park in Sealy. Take I-10 west from Houston to the second Sealy exit. Go north on Highway 36, and turn left at the light by the downtown bank. Go one block to the city park. About 50 miles from Houston.*

Exercise potential: *8*   **Scenery/Historical:**   *6*

Recommendations: *Not too far from Houston. Good roads, light traffic.*

Sealy - *In 1876 three leagues (over 13000 acres) of land were purchased from the San Felipe de Austin Town Corporation for the purpose of creating the new town of Sealy. San Felipe de Austin had previously been established 4 miles east of the site at which Sealy was to be built. John Sealy a banker and financier from Galveston provided his name for the city. For a number of years Sealy was the dividing point on the Santa Fe Railroad. The town had a round house and a machine shop to support the railroad operations. When many of the rail operations moved to Bellville many feared that the town would suffer a quick demise. It didn't happen because the town had other industries to support it. These other industries included a mattress factory, a broom factory, an oil mill, an ice works, three cotton gins, several blacksmiths and a grist mill.*

Of all these businesses, the most famous one is the mattress factory. Daniel Haynes developed a cotton mattress that was designed in such a way that it would not become tangled, tufted, or lumpy. By 1885 Mr. Haynes had developed machines for the manufacture of this mattress. In 1889 he received a patent on a revised machine and process. The Sealy Mattress Company adopted the trade name "Sealy" after it was purchased from Mr. Haynes. The business was later moved out of town.

The following item is from the Sealy Semi-Weekly newspaper, December 17, 1914.

F. Kallus --Merchant Tailor ..
Ready made clothing and Gents furnishings.

In these days of fine and cheap goods, first class workmen and general prosperity, there is no reason why any man should go poorly dressed. Some people insist that fine feathers don't make fine birds but they do to a great extent, just as a neat suit of clothes with the necessary accessories will put a good front on the poorest tramp. If you are not neatly dressed you cannot put up a brave front to the world for people will judge you by the clothes you wear, moralizers to the contrary notwithstanding.

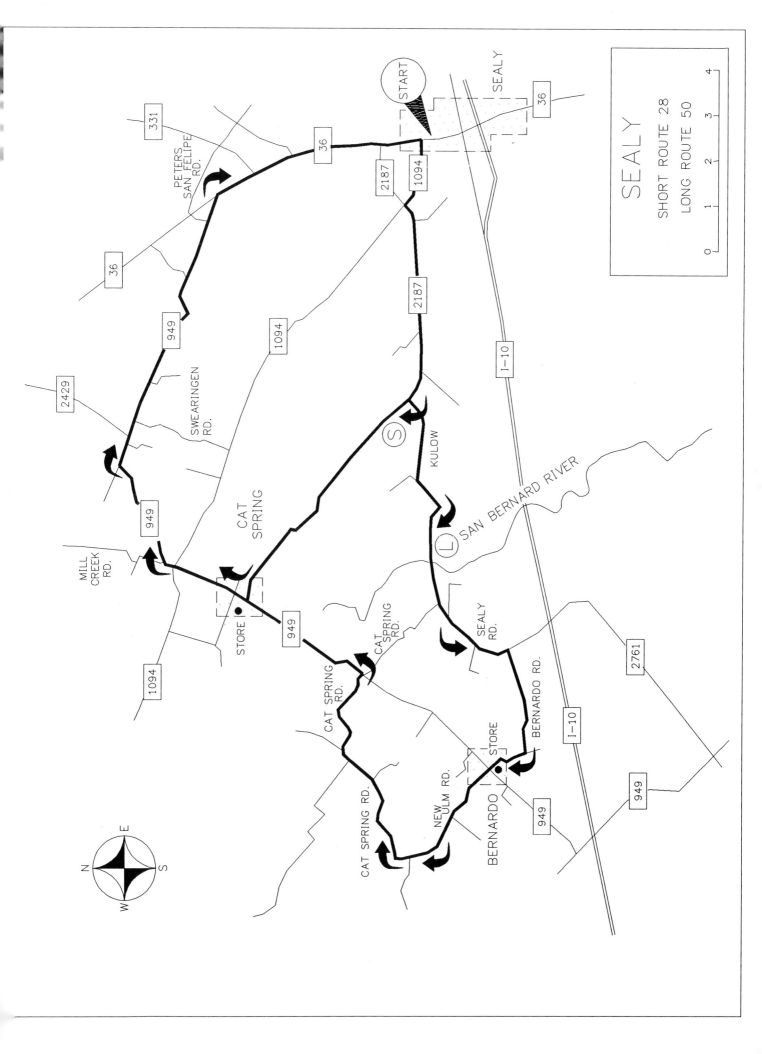

– STEPHEN F. AUSTIN STATE PARK –

Start: *Stephen F. Austin State Historical Park. Take I-10 west from Houston about 44 miles to the Stephen F. Austin Park exit. Go north on 1458 to the park (just before the Brazos River bridge).*

Exercise Potential: *7*   **Scenery/Historical:** *6*

Recommendations: *Relatively close to Houston. About an hour's drive from town. Low traffic on all roads except highway 36 (which has a wide shoulder).*

Stephen F. Austin State Historical Park - *is near the town of San Felipe. There's not much in the town now, but the place got started on the right foot. It was originally called San Felipe de Austin. Stephen F. Austin selected this place in July of 1823 to be his first colony in the area and Austin, himself, lived in a cabin in the area for four years. At the Stephen F. Austin Historical Park is a replica of Mr. Austin's home and a statue honoring Mr. Austin. Some of the bricks in the chimney are from the original house.*

Near the park a town hall was built (about 1830) in which were held the 1832 and 1833 conventions of the Mexican Department of Brazos. In addition, in 1835 a 'consultation' was held between the citizens of the area and the Mexican government in an attempt to resolve differences. The attempt failed and in 1835 the provisional government of the state was formed with Henry Smith as governor.

Stephen F. Austin Statue

In 1836 the Texas declaration of independence was adopted and the state government was moved from the site. In April of that year the entire town was burned as Sam Houston's army retreated to San Jacinto. General Houston wanted to make sure that there were no resources in San Felipe for the advancing Mexican army to use.

One of the more famous area plantations was the **Sunnyside Plantation.** *It was located north of Brookshire, west of what is now highway 359. Today, there is a turn in the road called Sunnyside Community (on the ride) named after the plantation. The end of slavery in Texas also ended the plantation operations. It was in a slave dwelling here that a black man was born who ultimately led the Texas delegation to the Republican National Convention in 1872.*

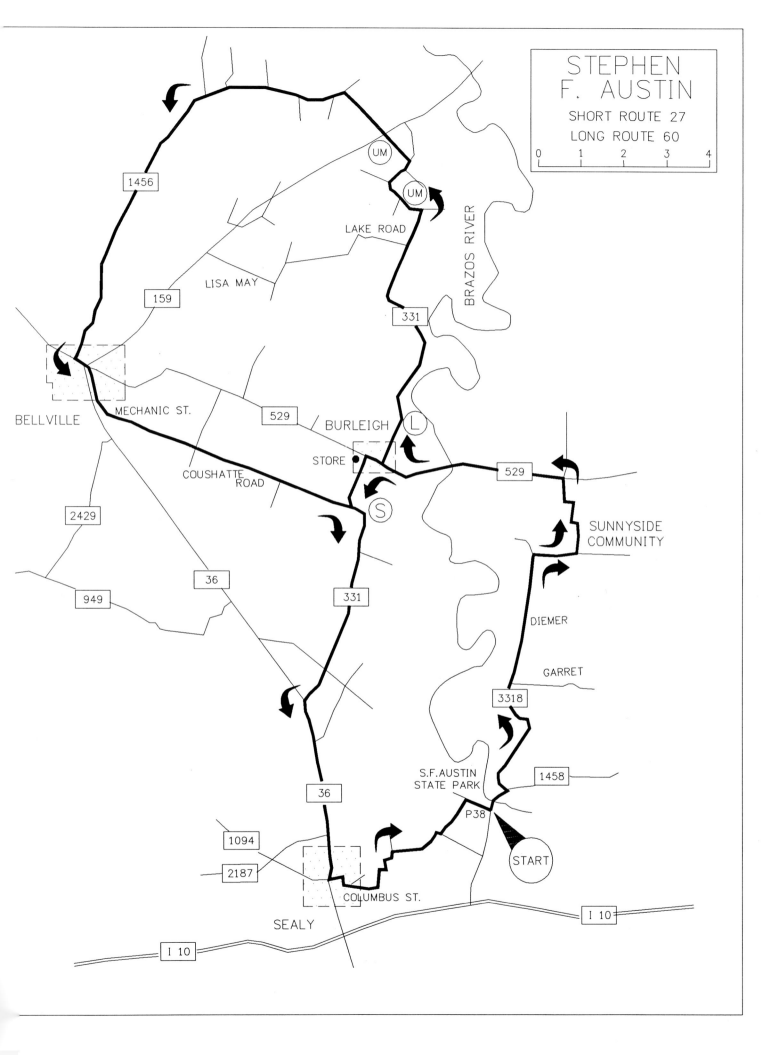

- Southwest -

– CRABB –

Start: *Park and Ride parking lot. Take the Southwest Freeway (Highway 59) south, cross the Brazos River and take the Highway 762 exit. Go south on 762 to the Park and Ride lot. About 30 miles from (downtown) Houston. Closer if you live on the southwest side of town.*

Exercise potential: *8*   **Scenery/Historical:** *4*

Recommendations: *This ride is near Houston and therefore it is convenient to get to when you don't have a lot of time available for a bike ride. The land here is flat and open and a ride here is best done in the winter, fall, or spring when the weather is a bit cooler. In the summer it can be tough.*

Crabb *- The area around Crabb was once part of the (Abner and Joseph) Kuykendall plantation. When Joseph Kuykendall died in 1878 his widow married a Mr. Crabb. The Crabb name was given to the town.*

Damon *- The town of Damon was built on land granted by Stephen F. Austin to Abraham Darst in 1829. Samuel Damon, who was in the business of producing brick for area homes and plantations, married the daughter of Mr. Darst and his name was taken for the name of the town.*

Damon's Mound is a limestone formation. The mound is about a mile long and a half a mile wide. The limestone in the formation rises to almost 100 feet above ground. Samuel Damon owned the property which contained the mound. Much of the limestone used in the construction of Houston buildings was taken from this mound.

H. L. & P. Power Plant

The Houston Lighting & Power Company power plant is visable for most of this ride through the flat coastal plain. Coal is brought in by train to power this plant. What looks like a small black hill on the gounds of the plant is, in fact, the coal supply for the plant.

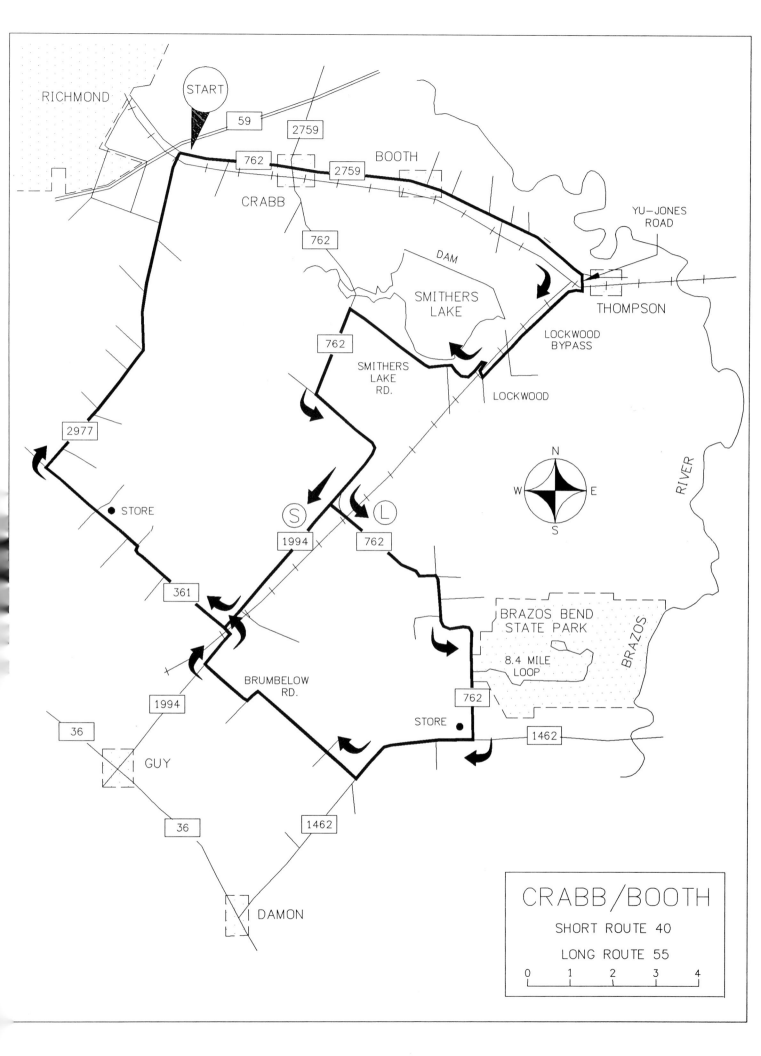

RICHMOND

START

59

2759

762

2759

BOOTH

CRABB

762

YU–JONES ROAD

DAM

SMITHERS LAKE

THOMPSON

762

SMITHERS LAKE RD.

LOCKWOOD BYPASS

LOCKWOOD

2977

STORE

N

W E

S

RIVER

361

S

1994

L

762

BRAZOS BEND STATE PARK

8.4 MILE LOOP

BRAZOS

1994

BRUMBELOW RD.

762

36

STORE

GUY

1462

36

1462

DAMON

CRABB/BOOTH

SHORT ROUTE 40

LONG ROUTE 55

0   1   2   3   4

- WEST OAKS -

Start: *Northwest corner of West Oaks Mall parking lot. Corner Westheimer (FM 1093) and Highway 6. About 20 miles from downtown Houston.*

Exercise potential: *7*   **Scenery/Historical:** *4*

Recommendations: *Good, quick ride. Close to Houston especially if you live on the Southwest side of town.*

Brazos River - *Most of this ride is in the Brazos River Valley so it is appropriate that we discuss the history of the river here.*

The full name of the river, often used in Spanish accounts of explorers and settlers is Brazos de Dios, --which translates literally as 'Arms of God'. There are several stories which are told which explain the origin of the name. One of the stories is that Francisco Vazquez de Coronado and his fellow travelers were about to die due to a shortage of fresh water when the Indians which lived in the area guided them to a small stream. De Coronado was so grateful to be delivered safely to the river that he named it Brazos de

Brazos River

Dios. Another story is that a Spanish ship was lost and the crew was without drinking water in the Gulf of Mexico. When the sailors spotted the river they sailed upstream to get to the point at which the water became fresh ..and they gave the river the name.

The river is unique in several ways. This is the longest (840 miles) river in the state of Texas and it is the river which empties the most water from the state. The longest branch of the river, the Double Mountain Fork begins in New Mexico but the contribution of water from New Mexico is small and the river can be considered to be wholly within the state of Texas for practical purposes.

The first settlement on the river was San Felipe de Austin (now known simply as San Felipe). It is at the Brazos that the first battle for Texas independence took place and at which (Washington-on-the-Brazos) there were established two of the first seats of government for the Republic of Texas.

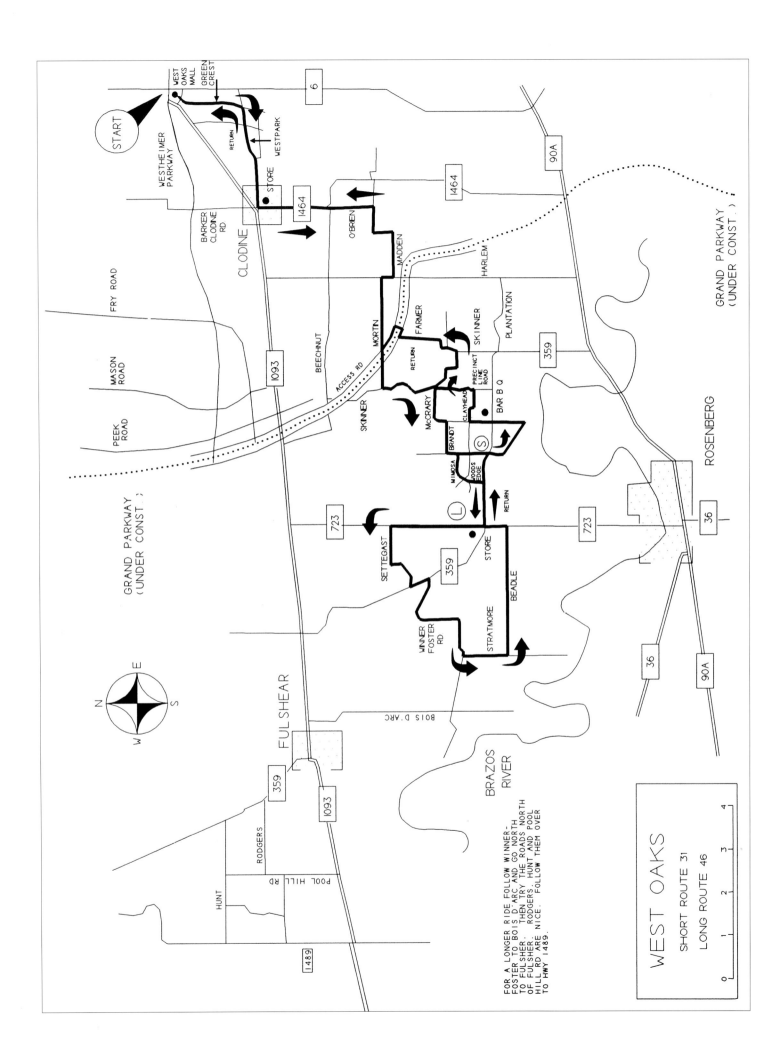

WEST OAKS

SHORT ROUTE 31
LONG ROUTE 46

FOR A LONGER RIDE FOLLOW WINNER-
FOSTER TO BOIS D'ARC AND GO NORTH
TO FULSHER. THEN TRY THE ROADS NORTH
OF FULSHER. RODGERS, HUNT AND POOL
HILL RD ARE NICE. FOLLOW THEM OVER
TO HWY 1489.

0   1   2   3   4

- South -

– DICKINSON –

Start: *Jack Brooks Park. Go south on I-45 about 40 miles. Take the Highway 1764, 2004, Texas City exit. After you exit the freeway, turn right. Quickly turn left (by the dog track) to get to 2004. On Highway 2004, turn right and continue to the park. There's parking available at the Veteran's Memorial Parking lot.*

Exercise potential: *8*   **Scenery/Historical:**   *3*

Recommendations: *This is a flat land ride over the coastal plains of the Texas gulf coast. There isn't much variation in the terrain to keep your interest, but this ride represents a good opportunity to get out on your bike and get a good exercise ride.*

Dickinson - *was once promoted as the greatest farming country in the world (a little bit of an overstatement) in brochures, handbills, and by salespeople in the Midwest. Dickinson and other cities along the Santa Fe Trail (highway 6) did manage to gain some recognition as agricultural areas. In fact, some promoters went so far as to call Dickinson "the strawberry capital of the world". It is true that in its prime Dickinson would ship 15 freight cars full of strawberries per year. Founded by Scotsman John Dickinson and later developed by General E. B. Nichols who fought beside Sam Houston in the Battle of San Jacinto, Dickinson grew rapidly during World War II. It was at that time that the industrialization of the area took place.*

Liverpool - *The site of a trading post before 1838. The town was founded in 1906 with the coming of the Louis, Brownsville, and Mexico Railroad.*

Alvin - *The character played by Dustin Hoffman in the movie "The Graduate" was "a little worried about his future". Alvin, Texas is like that. Alvie Morgan, an employee of the Santa Fe Railroad started the town in the late 1800's. Since then, the town has had its share of boom and bust cycles. A catalog of the booms would include the orange grove boom about 1900, the Cape Jasmine (sought after by the New York florists) boom, the strawberry boom, the rice farming boom, and finally (whew!) the oil boom. In addition to all of this, Alvin has had to survive a yellow fever epidemic (1897), two hurricanes (1900 and 1915), and a major fire (1902).*

There's a story they tell in this area. *The story was told best by Catherine Foster, a librarian by profession and a direct descendent of early Texas settlers, in her book "Ghosts Along the Brazos" (a collection of Brazoria County legends). A Mr. James Bailey settled on a plantation in Brazoria County about 1818. Mr Bailey could be a tough customer when he wanted to be, but he was known to be honest and trustworthy. Bailey died from a fever in 1832 and his will asked that he be buried standing up and facing west. This was done.*

His widow, however, did not follow through on one of his requests -- that a jug of whiskey be buried with him in his grave. Legend has it that the ghost of Bailey has roamed the prairie in search of that jug ever since. The ghost has taken the form of a brilliant ball of light. It was first seen in 1836 by the new resident of the Bailey property. The light has been chased, but never caught. Whenever anyone got close to the light it would disappear. In 1976 the light was seen again by two Angleton teachers. They said it resembled a motorcycle light, but it was in an area where no motorcycle could go.

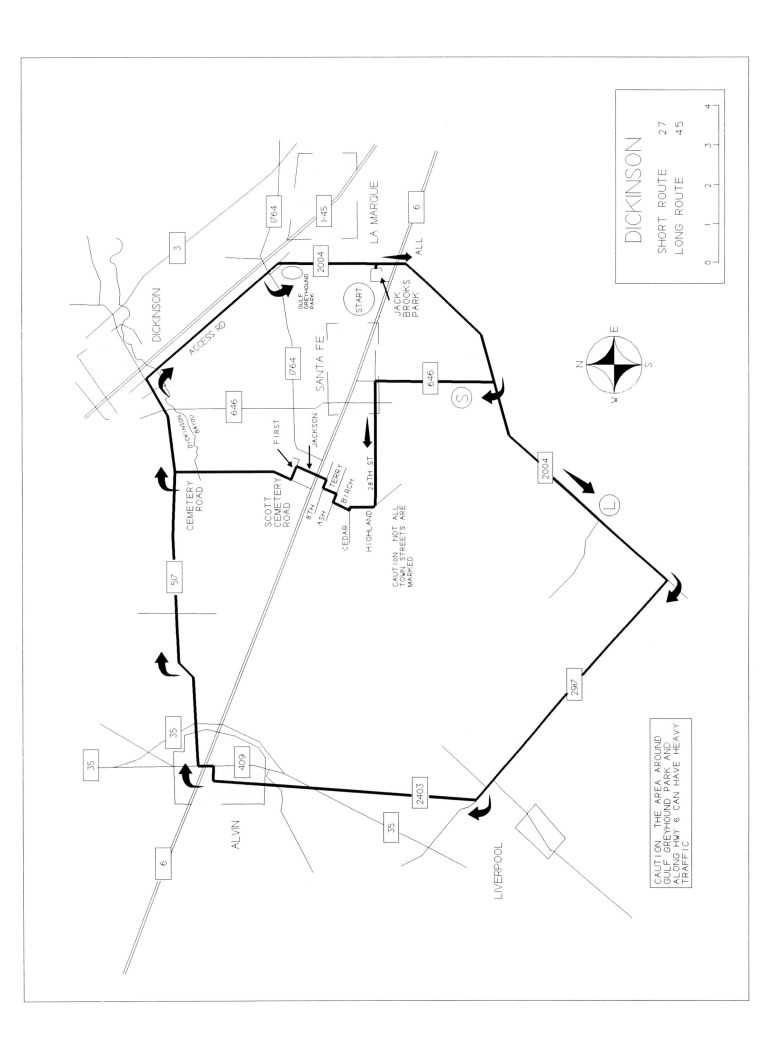

- GALVESTON -

Start : *Parking lot of Galvez Mall. If you're driving from Houston, take I-45 south about 55 miles and exit at Highway 61; do a U turn under the freeway to get to the Galvez Mall.*

Exercise potential: *4*   **Scenery/Historical:** *10*

Recommendations: *Start early on a Sunday morning to miss the heavy Seawall Blvd. traffic. Watch for railroad tracks in the roads --these tracks can grab your front wheel and cause you to take a nasty spill. Traffic on Broadway can be heavy. This ride is recommended as a slow, sight-seeing ride.*

Galveston - *the one-time home of Jean Lafitte, and probably the most interesting historical city in this book. For more information (there's a lot available) inquire at the Visitor's Center at 2016 Strand. (You'll pass it on the ride.)*

[1] Moody mansion - *acquired by the Moody family for 10 cents on the dollar after the 1900 hurricane.*

[2] Ashton Villa - *the oldest mansion on the island.*

[3] First Baptist Church - *built in 1958 and the 4th building to be occupied by the congregation.*

[4] Trinity Episcopal Church

[5] St. Mary's Cathedral - *corner 21st and Church - built in 1848, the oldest religious building in the city and the oldest cathedral in the state. Used as a refuge during the 1900 storm.*

[6] 1894 Opera House - *Greats who performed here include: Enrico Caruso, Oscar Wilde, John Philip Sousa, and Sara Bernhardt.*

Moody Mansion

[7] Lighthouse - *built in 1872 (now privately owned) and used as a refuge for 100 people when the storm of 1900 killed 6000 people on the island.*

Bolivar Lighthouse

[8] Fort Travis - *WW-II gun emplacements. During WW-II ten and twelve inch guns were at the ready here, but the Germans never attacked.*

[9] The Ashbel Smith building - *also known as "Old Red" - UT Campus, opened in 1891 for the 23 students who were attending.*

[10] Hendley Building - *Used as a lookout during the Civil War. The Confederate troops could observe the Union gunboats in their efforts to blockade the harbor.*

[11] Shern Moody Plaza - *The Center for Transportation and Commerce Train depot at the end of the Strand (25th street)*

[12] Avenue L Baptist Church - *Oldest Black Baptist Church in Texas.*

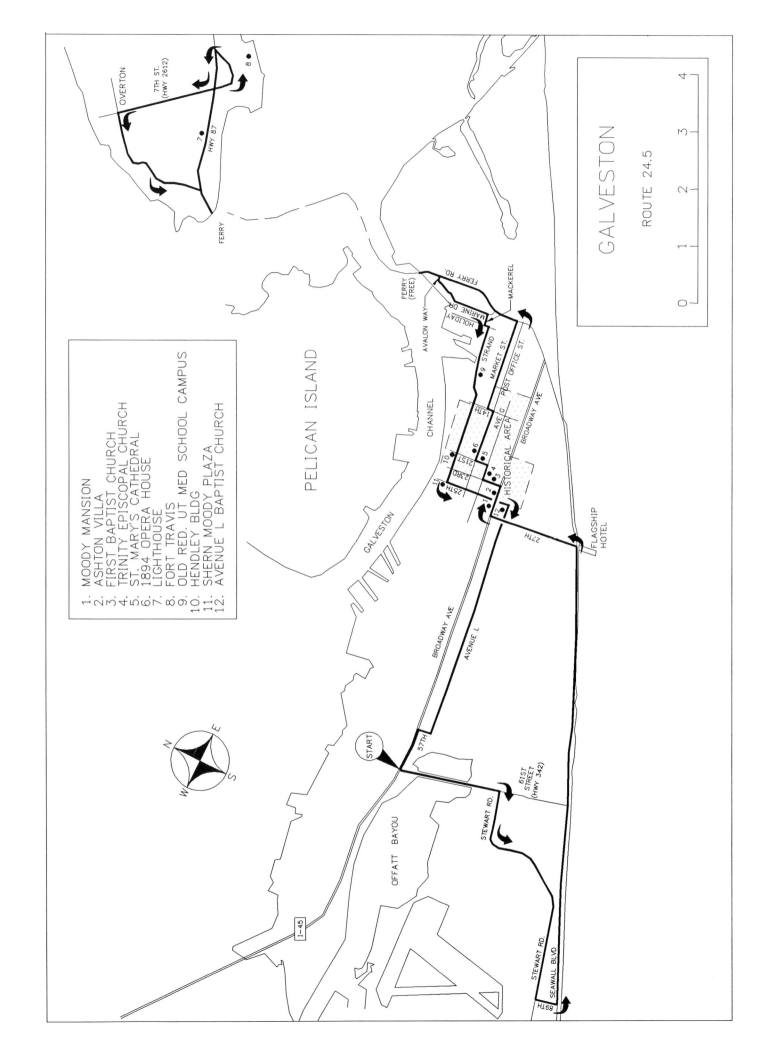

GALVESTON

ROUTE 24.5

0   1   2   3   4

1. MOODY MANSION
2. ASHTON VILLA
3. FIRST BAPTIST CHURCH
4. TRINITY EPISCOPAL CHURCH
5. ST. MARY'S CATHEDRAL
6. 1894 OPERA HOUSE
7. LIGHTHOUSE
8. FORT TRAVIS
9. OLD RED. UT MED SCHOOL CAMPUS
10. HENDLEY BLDG
11. SHERN MOODY PLAZA
12. AVENUE L BAPTIST CHURCH

PELICAN ISLAND

GALVESTON

CHANNEL

OFFATT BAYOU

START

BROADWAY AVE

AVENUE L

57TH

STEWART RD.

61ST STREET (HWY 342)

STEWART RD.

SEAWALL BLVD

89TH

FLAGSHIP HOTEL

27TH

BROADWAY AVE

HISTORICAL AREA

POST OFFICE ST.

AVE. G

14TH

21ST

23RD

25TH

MARKET ST.

STRAND

MACKEREL

FERRY RD.

MARINE DR.

HOLIDAY

AVALON WAY

FERRY (FREE)

FERRY

OVERTON

7TH ST. (HWY 2612)

HWY 87

I-45

- East -

- LIBERTY -

Start: *Town of Liberty. From Houston, take I-10 East to State Highway 90. Continue eastbound on Highway 90 to Liberty. About a 45 mile drive from Houston.*

Exercise potential: *7*   **Scenery/Historical:** *7*

Recommendations: *This is a nice ride especially suitable for riders who live on the east side of Houston. The terrain is flat to gently rolling.*

Liberty - *Originally the area around Liberty was settled by Spaniards. The Mexican government made this area attractive to new settlement by giving land and tax abatements to these settlers.*

The Liberty Bell tower is on the corner of Milam and Sam Houston Streets (behind the museum). The bell was the first one cast from the mold which created the Liberty Bell. In 1976 Liberty was a national Bicentennial City and the tower housing the bell in Liberty was completed in that year.

Daisetta - *was built (est. 1917) to service the oil field in the surrounding area. The town was named for Daisy Barrett and Etta White.*

Who would have thought that the sleepy area around Liberty could become the site for a death by firearm? The story is suitable for a daytime television drama. The fact that this story is real and that you'll be cycling in the area makes the tale particularly interesting.

Liberty Bell Tower

Price Daniel Jr. was the son of a former Governor of Texas. One day he strolled into the Dairy Queen in Liberty (look for it on your way out of town) and was served by the woman who was to become his wife and who was to be accused of his murder. On January 19, 1981, Price and Vicki Daniel argued. When Price Daniel threatened the life of Vicki, she picked up a gun and fired what she called at her trial a "warning shot". Beyond that, she testified, she had no recollection of firing a shot that penetrated Price Daniel's aorta and caused him to bleed to death before help could arrive. Price Daniel Jr. died at his home (the home was previously the home of Governor Price Daniel Sr.) on FM 1011 (also known as Governor's Road). FM 1011 is on the ride.

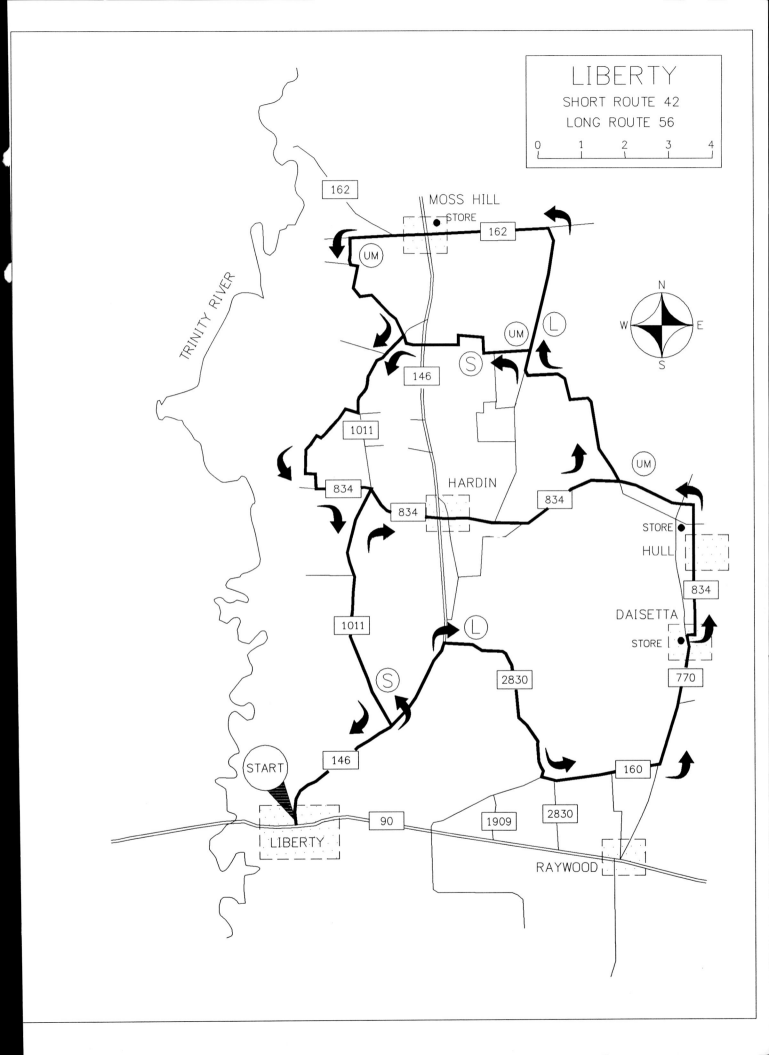

The Texas Bicycle Map Company brings you *Texas!!!*

Bicycling the Houston Area

...25 maps with rides in and around Houston. Four in-town rides (including the Houston Heights and River Oaks), a ride in historic Galveston, and rides in the beautiful gulf coast area surrounding Houston. You'll start rides in Conroe, Brenham (home of Blue Bell Ice Cream), Chappell Hill, Bellville, Brookshire, Columbus, Katy, New Ulm, Liberty, and more! The 'yellow book' as Houstonians have come to know *Bicycling the Houston Area* has been extremely popular and has opened up new territory to cyclists in southeast Texas.

Bicycling the Texas Hill Country and West Texas

...29 maps (in the revised edition) with rides in the beautiful Texas Hill Country, in Austin, in San Antonio, and in challenging West Texas. There's no better riding anywhere in Texas than in the beautiful Texas Hill Country. The roads are wide and smooth, the traffic count is low, and the scenery is great. In addition to the new rides in Austin and San Antonio, you can start rides in New Braunfels, Wimberly, Kerrville, Fredericksburg, Leaky, Alpine, and Fort Davis. This book also includes two 3-day tours.

Bicycling the Dallas-Fort Worth Area

...25 maps for rides in and around Dallas and Fort Worth. Get your copy of this new book containing rides from Aledo, from Tyler (the Beauty and the Beast Ride), around Benbrook Lake, from Crowley, from Granbury, around Joe Pool Lake, around Lake Lavon, near Lake Tawakoni, in Las Colinas, from Lewisville, from Mineral Wells, from Palo Pinto, from Rockwall, from Waxahachie, and more. The northeast corner of the state offers some excellent cycling, and this book tells you where to find it.

Mountain Bicycling the Houston Area

Got yourself a mountain bicycle? Well, even if there are no mountains in Houston, there are plenty of places to ride your mountain bicycle. How about a spin through Memorial Park (along what is known as the Ho Chi Minh trail) or along Braes Bayou? Out of town, there are rides in Brazos Bend State Park, in Cat Spring, Bellville and Chappell Hill. Get the most out of your mountain bicycle... try some (or all!) the rides in this great book.